'A' LE
NOTES FOR
ENDURING LOVE BY
IAN MCEWAN

Joe Broadfoot &

David Broadfoot

First published in 2012

by Londinium Publishing Limited

13 Hereford Gardens, London SE13 5LU

ISBN-13: 978-1477551080
ISBN-10: 1477551085

ACKNOWLEDGMENTS

We would like to thank the following people for their help and support: our friends, work and school colleagues and all the family, particularly Jean Thompson.

CONTENTS

Introduction   6

Chapter 1   15

Chapter 2   20

Chapter 3   23

Chapter 4   26

Chapter 5   29

Chapter 6   32

Chapter 7   35

Chapter 8   38

Chapter 9   41

Chapter 10   44

Chapter 11   47

Chapter 12   49

Chapter 13   52

Chapter 14   55

Chapter 15   59

Chapter 6   63

Chapter 17   66

Chapter 8   70

Chapter 9   75

Chapter 10   79

Chapter 21   85

Chapter 22   90

Chapter 23   96

Chapter 24   99

Appendices   104

Glossary   108

Brief Introduction

This book is aimed at 'A' Level students of English Literature who are studying Ian McEwan's *Enduring Love*. The focus will be on what examiners are looking for and, here you will find each chapter and the appendices covered in detail. We hope this will help you and be a valuable tool in your studies and revision.

Criteria for high marks

Make sure you use appropriate critical language (see glossary of literary terms at the back). You need your argument to be fluent, well-structured and coherent. Stay focused!

Analyse and explore the use of form, structure and the language. Explore how these aspects affect the meaning.

Make connections between texts and look at different interpretations. Explore their strengths and weaknesses. Don't forget to use supporting references to strengthen your argument.

Analyse and explore the context.

Best essay practice

Use PEE for your paragraphs: point/evidence/explain.

Other tips

Make your studies active!

Don't just sit there reading! Never forget to annotate, annotate and annotate! It is important for you to make your own notes on following:

Characterisation: look at Joe, Clarissa, Jed, John Logan, Jean Logan and Inspector Linley, in particular.

Themes: obsession, love (in the Indicator version of 'La Belle Dame Sans Merci', John Keats uses romantic conventions to show that idealized love often leads to alienation and despair, does McEwan do something similar?), selfishness v altruism (for instance, does Jean represent the 'selfish gene' as described by Richard Dawkins?), science, reading, stories and storytelling, knowledge and truth, gender and sexuality, and last but not least, endings.

Setting/place: Logan's house, field, police station, restaurant, North Downs and Joe and Clarissa's flat.

Narrative: non-linear structure, unreliable narrator, tenses, chronological narrative time, restricted narrator, first-person narrator, figurative language, scientific and religious discourse, dialogue, direct speech, and denouement.

PEE Example

Write a PEE paragraph for each of the above, plus a bullet point list of quotes for each aspect of narrative.

For example, on the theme of obsession:

Point: There are at least two obsessions driving the plot of Enduring Love: Jed's stalking of Joe taking centre stage, with Clarissa's obsessive interest with the poet, John Keats, providing an interesting parallel as a sub-plot.

Evidence: Jed deludes himself into believing his feelings for Joe are mutual, whereas Clarissa seems to suffer similar delusions induced by her obsession with Keats, believing in a lost love letter despite a distinct lack of supporting evidence.

Explain: The theme of obsession illustrates McEwan's point that religion, represented by Jed, can be an act of faith spilling into delusion if left unchecked; while art, represented by Clarissa, is similarly guilty.

Exam Guidance

You are allowed to use the book in the exam, but it must un-annotated!

Looking at some past AQA exam papers there is some regularity about the type of questions you will be asked to answer on *Enduring Love*. It's in Section A of the paper and you're expected to spend 30 minutes each on 2 questions.

Twenty-one points are up for grabs so make sure you get key terms across to earn you those marks! Check the glossary for appropriate terms.

The other 21 marks are for answering a question, which also can be related to narrative techniques. This is more about your opinion on one aspect of McEwan's style. Make sure you keep your argument balanced and argue both sides before concluding.

One recent question was about Enduring Love's seeming preoccupation with 'how stories can be constructed'. This can lead to a discussion of McEwan's **self-conscious narrative** techniques.

Another recent question focused on **characterisation**. This question was about the readers' sympathy for Joe. Rather than discussing all McEwan's narrative techniques, make sure you focus on the character for this kind of question.

We spotted another exam question asking about the **intertextuality** of the novel. Again, it relates to narrative techniques to a point, but here the focus is on the importance of McEwan's 'use of other texts (i.e. scientific, literary and religious)' to the 'whole' novel. Make sure you argue both points of view, if possible. On the one hand, you can say these digressions slow the plot down and are detrimental to the novel's effectiveness as a thriller, in that sense. On the plus side, you could also say it adds some academic interest and allows the reader to draw historical and Biblical parallels between Joe, Wordsworth and Adam, for example.

The first question asks you to describe McEwan's **narrative methods** within a specific chapter. In recent years, chapters 5, 10, 12, 14 and 19 have appeared in exam papers. Spend 30 minutes answering this.

The second question asks your opinion on one of the following: **characterisation** (e.g. Joe and Jed's relationship, Joe), **plot** (e.g. surprise elements), **intertextuality** or another aspect of narrative. For this question, you will be asked to look at the novel as a whole. Spend 30 minutes answering this question.

Other aspects of narrative

Significance of place: (e.g. the pathetic fallacy of the oak tree in the opening). If you think setting symbolically evokes a specific emotion, then it is an example of objective correlative (a term devised by T.S. Elliot).

Arrangement of time: Also look at the era/period.

Point Of View: Look at the narrator's ideology, his proximity to action, the impact of narrator, shifting perspectives and competing viewpoints.

Voices In Text: Focus on what the narrator sounds like and how his voice is created. Look at direct speech, attribution and indirect speech, in particular.

Destination: reading the novel as a journey and asking what the reader learns or experiences and exploring various interpretations.

Philosophical Context

The three main protagonists have radically different views on life. Philosophically, Joe stands for reason, Clarissa for emotion and Jed for religion. The rationalist and scientific stance, represented by Joe, has been the dominant force in Western culture since the eighteenth-century Enlightenment. However, Romanticism, represented by Clarissa, made significant inroads at the turn of the nineteenth century, reasserting the importance of the following: heroes and anti-heroes, national identity, nature, innocence, individualism and symbolism amongst other things. Faith, represented by Jed, has been in decline generally since the Renaissance.

Literary Context

John Keats: this Romantic poet is undoubtedly the most important literary figure in *Enduring Love*. His alleged meeting with his idol, William Wordsworth, which is documented within the novel, is particularly significant as Keats appears to be Jed's Gothic double (167-8).

Keats was an admirer of the middle-aged Wordsworth, at the time. Although it may be a different kind of admiration, nevertheless the parallels between the two poets and Jed and Joe are obvious. Amongst other things, the age differences between the real-life historical characters and the fictional ones are extremely close.

There is also another aspect: that of the unreliable narrator. The artist Benjamin Haydon, who introduced the two poets to each other, claimed that Wordsworth described Keats's work as 'pretty'. The latter took it as an insult, yet the former meant it as a complement. It is a good example of misreading, one of the themes of *Enduring Love*.

There are also the references in the restaurant scene to Keats's *Endymion* and 'Ode on a Grecian Urn'. The ode's binary oppositions of: transience versus permanence, joy versus pain, nature versus art, and knowledge versus imagination are repeated in *Enduring Love*; and the ode's closing line is quoted: 'Beauty is truth, truth beauty (166). Meanwhile, *Endymion* is sometimes regarded as similar to *Enduring Love* as both works feature extended digressions and narrative expositions. There is a distinct parallel between the closing line of the novel, which is 'faith is joy', and the opening words of *Endymion Book I* : 'A thing of beauty is a joy for ever'.

The similarities between the poet and Jed continue on a personal level, with Keats fearing his love of Fanny Brawne was unrequited. Although Jed believes his love of Joe is returned, he is mistaken. Also, like Keats, Jed suffers from an illness. Keats contracts tuberculosis and dies young, while Jed is suffering from de Clérambault's syndrome.

Other relevant works:

Ian McEwan: *The Comfort of Strangers* (1981), The *Child in Time* (1987), *Atonement* (2001)

John Milton – *Paradise Lost* (1667)

Stephen Hawking – *A Brief History of Time* (1988)

Steven Pinker – *The Language Instinct* (1994)

Richard Dawkins – *The Selfish Gene* (1976)

Other relevant writers:

William Wordsworth (1770-1850)

George Gordon Byron (1788-1824)

Percy Bysshe Shelley (1792-1822)

William Blake (1757-1827)

Samuel Taylor Coleridge (1772-1834)

Anna Laetitia Barbauld (1743-1825)

Cultural context

- **Evolutionary psychology** – Darwinian natural selection and how it influences behaviour.

- **Humanity and animality** – see the Genome Project – examples in the novel include Joe defecating in the woods and Leo wearing face paint to look like a tiger.

- **Sociobiology** - expounded by E.O. Wilson which, amongst other things, suggests the incest taboo exists to prevent the unhealthy cross-fertilisation of genes.

- **Kin selection** – William Hamilton claims that siblings will sacrifice themselves for genetic reasons.

- **Language is inherent** – see Steven Pinker.

- **Emotion affects reason** – see Antonio Damasio.

- **Altruism** – has a firm genetic basis, according to Robert Wright, a game theorist.

Now let us look at the novel. Page references are from the paperback edition, published by Vintage Books in 2006. Words that the examiners may be looking for are written in **bold**.

CHAPTER 1

Looking at the first page, it's the names that jump off the page at you. The name 'Clarissa' gets two mentions, so it must be important! And it certainly is from an **intertextual** perspective.

The thing to note is Clarissa is a very literary name. Samuel Richardson's *Clarissa* (1748) immediately comes to mind. Richardson was an eminent writer of the eighteen century who also wrote *Pamela* (1740), which was lampooned by Henry Fielding's burlesque entitled, *Shamela* (1741). The important thing about Richardson's aforementioned two novels is their **epistolary** structure. To some extent, by alluding to Richardson's work McEwan is warning us to expect a lot of letters and correspondence in this novel also.

However, McEwan begins his book with a carefully planned picnic, which effectively brings together the two lovers: Joe Rose and his girlfriend, Clarissa.

Food has often been linked with sexuality by novelists. For instance, Gustave Flaubert in *Madame Bovary* uses food images to make a similar point, as does the aforementioned Fielding in *Tom Jones*.

The other name that leaps quickly into view when picking up the novel is Mas de Daumas Gassac, a wine producer from France. The lovers are enjoying a 1987 bottle of Daumas Gassac, which instantly dates the novel. Notice, throughout the novel, the repeated references to France, French people and inanimate objects from France. Interestingly, 1987 was not a particularly good vintage for this brand of wine. It makes one wonder why McEwan felt it worth a mention. Was he trying to say that Joe, the first-person narrator, is a snob, who can't tell the difference between good wine and average wine? If so, he's setting Joe up to be an unreliable narrator, who can't be trusted.

Yet the narrative is tense. **Syntactically**, short sentences like: 'I ran faster' (1) ensure it has a breathless quality right from the start. We, as readers, can sense the drama. Long sentences juxtaposed against short ones, increase the tension later in the chapter: 'A mighty fist socked the balloon in two rapid blows, one-two, the second more vicious than the first. And the first was vicious.'

We also feel that the outcome of whatever drama is to follow will be negative. The appearance of a buzzard **foreshadows** death, for this is a bird that feeds on carrion as well as small helpless mammals. It's interesting that the narrator states that he sees 'through the eyes' (1) of this bird of prey, almost as if he's partially to blame for the casualties to come. Coincidentally, sheep farmers often unfairly blame buzzards for killing their lambs, when the truth is the birds are simply feeding on an already dead one! The blame game is a theme throughout this novel and this is firmly and subtly established from the off.

The next thing to notice about the opening chapter is its **self-conscious** tone. The narrator admits he's 'holding back, delaying the information' (2). The artifices of the novelist are being revealed to the reader, which makes this novel typical of **post-modernist fiction**. This forces the audience to become **active** rather than passive readers as they are being forced to think about how the narrative is being presented to them rather than being completely sucked into the story.

Now let's look at the chapter in more detail. The opening line: 'The beginning is simple to mark' (1) shows that the narrative is **retrospective**.

The 'turkey oak' (1) reference symbolises peace and serenity but could be interpreted as generically belonging to the **bucolic** or **pastoral Romantic genre**. The oak is an example of **pathetic fallacy** because it is an inanimate object actively protecting Joe and Clarissa from the wind. The oak has come to life!

The wine they are drinking indicates class and the narrator's recollection of the name proves Joe has a vivid memory. 'We turned to look' (1) marks a **shift in tone and tempo** as the focus switches to action without the minute details that marked the beginning. The narrative builds tension by starting slowly and quickening the pace.

The picnic **setting** could be a prelapsarian Eden. Joe and Clarissa eat under a tree, like the Biblical Adam and Eve eating from the Tree of Knowledge. Jed could be the serpent or snake in this interpretation. John Logan's fall from the balloon parallels man's 'fall from innocence'. The opening lines mentioning 'the beginning' (1) echoes the start of The Book of Genesis from the Old Testament.

What follows is an example of **shifting perspective**, as the narrative focus switches from Joe to the buzzard soaring above. The buzzard should be more accurate, **omniscient** and distant than Joe, who is involved and fuelled by adrenalin and therefore **unreliable**.

'Parry and I were tiny forms' (2) from a buzzard's eye view shows that this perspective is god-like, making the people beneath appear insignificant in their 'puny human distress' (2). The description of the aftermath as 'the second crop' (2) can be interpreted as religious in tone, as it could relate to a Biblical harvest.

Then the narrator becomes quite **self-conscious,** 'delaying the information' (2). This narrative style allows the audience to read **ironically** with a critical **distance**, rather than naïvely. Later, the narrator uses filmic language to achieve the same effect: 'let me freeze the frame' (12).

Chronologically, the narrative in the chapter moves from the **retrospective**, a few minutes before the accident to even further back in time earlier in the day, at Heathrow (3-5), before moving back to the Chiltern Hills (5). The almost cinematic return of the 'buzzard' brings the characters back to where they started before the **flashback**.

The buzzard 'soaring, circling and dipping in the tumult of currents' (1) above the Chiltern Hills evokes a certain sublimity, associated with Romantic artists, poets and novelists. Later, we encounter a Romantic poet in the shape of John Keats (6). **Romanticism** tended to emphasise, sometimes through **personification** as in this case, the raw power of Nature and, in this chapter, the wind's 'rage' (9) causes John's death. Romanticism also emphasised the heroic, and Joe attempts to be a hero, declaring it was 'his duty to hang on' to the rope (13).

The **tone** is generally confessional and it sounds like the narrator is being interviewed. **Semantically**, the narrator's **lexical field** is mathematical and scientific, for instance, 'comforting geometry' (2) and 'ruthless gravity' (16). Note McEwan use of adjectives that relate to emotions, alongside the emotionless nouns. For people that dislike mathematics, 'comforting geometry' would be an **oxymoron**! There is also evidence of dramatic language, for instance, 'drama' and 'fifty theatrical happy endings' (4).

CHAPTER 2

The first thing to note about chapter 2 is the **self-conscious** narrative technique. 'Best to slow down' indicates the narrator is illuminating the artifice of storytelling. The **register** is **informal** and without the use of a subject, the opening **syntax** seems almost like a 'Wish you were here' postcard (17). Through **repetition**, 'I've already marked the beginning', the narrative continues to draw attention to itself (17).

Alongside this self-consciousness and informality, the **semantic field** continues to be scientific and mathematical , with terms like 'velocity', 'vertiginous theories' and 'Euclidean geometry' appearing (17). When in doubt, the narrator seems to cling on to the idea that science and mathematics can provide all the answers.

France is a **motif** that recurs throughout the novel, so we should not overlook the French word 'déjà vu' (18). Perhaps, this motif is not obviously significant in itself, yet the use of it does give the narrative more **coherence**. French words and products, like the wine at the beginning of chapter 1, do give the reader a sense that the narrator has a sense of class. He clearly likes the good things in life, so it tells us something about his character.

The dog **motif** also relates to **characterization** , but rather than describing Joe Rose, the narrator, it is applied to Jed Parry, who is described as 'a dog about to be punished' (20). Jed is described physically as 'all bones and sinew' like 'a pale Indian brave' with a 'habit of making a statement on the rising inflection of a question' (24). From Joe's perspective, Jed appears to lack answers to the questions he poses perhaps like the religion he represents.

The narrative becomes **self-conscious** once more when the narrator describes himself as 'in a dream' where he 'was both first and third persons' (19). This effectively works as a flashback to the buzzard's **omniscient** view in chapter 1. It shows that Joe is trying to be a **reliable narrator** by distancing himself from the action. Yet he is emotionally entangled, so cannot trust himself entirely. In the circumstances, he is unable to be coldly analytical like a scientist or mathematician.

During times of emotional crisis, Joe clings on to what he knows: science and mathematics. He relies on a relatively recent technological invention, a 'mobile phone' to call the emergency services. He seems to associate the phone with death, calling it 'the dense little slab' which makes it appear to resemble a gravestone (20) . This could be interpreted as showing Joe's **ambivalence** towards science.

Cinematic language follows, as Joe describes his situation in screenwriter-speak: 'I was in a soap opera . . . . It was intimacy, a tight two-shot' (21). This helps the reader picture the scene. Later, Joe makes an **allusion** to visual art again, when graphically describing John's corpse as: a 'Picassoesque violation of perspective' (23). Pablo Picasso helped to develop Cubism, which was all about analysing objects in terms of shapes. It is interesting that the narrator refers to Picasso, as like the famous artist, Joe has an analytic mind. Hence, the subtle **parallel** is part of Joe's characterization. Similarly, the 'Keystone Kops' reference to the police suggests Joe has little respect for them. The silent movie stars who called themselves the Keystone Kops portrayed an incompetent police force and were popular comedians in the early part of the twentieth century. Once again, the narrative uses filmic language to help readers picture the scene while offering information about Joe's character.

We start to question Joe's sanity when he says: 'I did not trust my balance' (21). Ostensibly, he means he did not feel steady on his feet, but it could also be a **pun**, indicating an unstable state of mind. Clarissa wants to slap him later and tell him to 'slow down', so it seems emotion has raced away with his reason (21). Yet just before that, he proudly narrates that his 'feet were anchored to the ground' (19). He seems to be deluding himself and downplaying the importance of emotion by stating that Clarissa's tears are 'no more than fact' (19).

The language becomes almost **theatrical** as Joe foreshadows Jed's 'long winter of . . . obsession' (21). This phrase is slightly reminiscent of William Shakespeare's line in Richard III that starts with: 'Now is the winter of our discontent'.

We also get some subtle indications about Jed's character as we see him voyeuristically 'watching' Joe(19). His portrayal as a homosexual is somewhat stereotypical as we see him with his 'hands resting on his hips' (23).

CHAPTER 3

The first thing to note about chapter 3 is the **setting**. The description is precise and unchanging, most exemplified by 'the railway clock above the door' (28). The narrator seems to take comfort in describing the scene in minute, almost scientific, detail. He even mentions 'a note left by the cleaning lady the day before' (28).

He then mentions 'the familiar weight of the wine glasses' which links cleverly with the preceding balloon disaster (28). Of course, a lack of weight pulling down the ropes has led to John Logan's death. It could be argued that there is even a link between alcohol consumption and John's demise if wine induced Joe to let go of the rope too soon. While the identity of the 'guilty party' is never identified, we as readers may draw our own conclusions from the narrative's array of clues.

The emotional recounting of the story begins, as Clarissa tells 'the beginning of her story in a rush' giving the reader a different **narrative perspective** (29). Her love of literature comes through as she quotes John Milton's *Paradise Lost* giving the narrative **intertextuality**: '*Hurl'd headlong flaming from th'Ethereal Sky*' (29). This use of language is **hyperbolic**, as John Logan may have plunged from the sky, but he certainly was not 'flaming'.

Yet for all his scientific values, Joe is equally unable to resist injecting guilty emotion into the narrative, showing Clarissa 'the rope burn' on his hands (29). After finishing off the bottle of 1987 Daumas Gassac, that links the present kitchen scene to the balloon accident, Joe reaches for a 'bottle of Beaujolais' (29). Alcohol, as well as emotion, is fuelling the narrative that Joe and Clarissa are composing together and that in itself suggests **unreliability**.

Emotion, of course, is much revered in **Romanticism**, a movement which the Keates-loving Clarissa knows all about. **Gothic novels** were born out of Romanticism and interestingly, McEwan uses the typically Gothic term 'unspeakable' to describe the writing process. He also uses terminology from the **semantic field** of construction to describe how he and Clarissa merge narratives 'like dedicated craftsmen at work, grinding the jagged edge of memories, hammering the unspeakable into forms of words' (30). For more evidence of the Gothic genre, notice when Clarissa acknowledges 'some unspoken thought' (32).

It shows how shaken Joe is that he is now using Gothic terminology instead of scientific words 'content to escape' his 'own feelings' (32). He has already used the semantic field of incarceration to describe how the single narratives started as 'prisoners in a cell' (29). As the two narratives blend together Joe describes it thus: 'Slowly our prison grew larger' (30).

Despite the growing synergy of their respective narratives, Joe stops short when it comes to embracing Clarissa's beliefs, firmly rejecting her idea that John's death 'must mean something' (32). He effectively reasserts his atheism, saying 'people sometimes suffered and died, not because their goodness was being tested, but precisely because there was nothing, no one, to test it. No one but us' (32).

After merging narratives under the influence of alcohol, the pair now reassert their differences. Using a virtual **oxymoron**, Clarissa says to Joe: 'You're so rational sometimes you're like a child . . .' (33). Joe questions it, but for the reader it serves to highlight the two character's ideological differences. After they make love, Joe describes himself as 'blessed' (33). This sudden use of religious terminology suggests that physicality may be one way of bridging intellectual differences. It is interesting that he uses a term that Jed would approve of. Joe later describes his love-making with Clarissa as 'deliverance', which is yet another religious term (34).

The story-telling process is once again discussed, firstly with Clarissa revealing her **backstory**, which explains her sudden 'shivering' (34). She reminisces about her uncle, who was 'shaking violently' after her cousin went missing (35). Joe replies with a story about his own nerves, but what it really reveals is that neither character can be completely trusted. Nerves will shape their narratives.

Another development about story-telling is revealed: the more times a tale is told, the less it affects the teller emotionally. Joe admits '[i]t became possible to recount the events [about the balloon accident] without re-living them in the faintest degree, without even remembering them' (36).

CHAPTER 4

The first thing to note about chapter 4 is the **allusion** or reference to **Romantic poetry** and more specifically to one particular Romantic poet, Leigh Hunt (38). Although Joe is discussing Clarissa's work commitments initially, some Romanticism filters through into his own narrative, when he refers to 'heroism' and a 'noble urge' (38).

Nevertheless, the **semantic field** continues to be mathematical at times, with the narrator refusing to blame the Hubble telescope's failure on 'some algorithmic arcane in the software' (39).

Despite Joe's pragmatism, his emotional state is making him an **unreliable narrator**. He admits: 'I suppose I was still in shock' (40). It even transforms itself into 'an unreliable urge to crap' (40). Maybe he is being subtly disparaging about the process of constructing a narrative. If that is indeed the case, then it is an example of **metafiction**. This seems likely as, in the next paragraph, the narrator discusses the 'storytelling' skills of nineteenth-century scientists, like Charles Darwin (41).

The scientific discussion moves on to 'anthropomorphism'. This is another form of metafiction, as it self-consciously reveals how narratives are erroneously formed even in science. Seeking to explain the behaviour of a dog, the anonymous letter writer featured in '*Nature* dated 1904' thought the animal tricked its master and then wore 'a look of undisguised triumph' (41). Joe is disparaging of such narratives, calling the account 'nonsense' (41). Interestingly, Jed is also compared to a dog in chapter two (20).

Despite his rational explanation of this incident, when it comes to his own life, Joe is ready to jump to conclusions. He assumes that the 'invisible' person 'behind the magazine rack' in the London Library is Jed (42). Yet all Joe sees is 'a flash of a white shoe and something red' (42). It is enough for Joe to make a leap of faith and believe he is being stalked. This is hardly the appliance of scientific principles, which require evidence before proceeding to a conclusion. Interestingly, the red may symbolise the blood of Christ and the white the body. Given Jed's religion, that would make sense.

Joe's religion is science and here he is the London Library trying to escape into a safe world of theory. Yet, his emotions are taking over. He finds that language is inadequate when it comes to expressing his feelings. This inadequacy is typically found in **Gothic** novels. He becomes quite poetic, using an **ascending tricolon** to express himself: 'I possessed a thought, a feeling, a sensation' (43). He adds: 'I was looking for its word' (43).

Joe returns to the comfort of his normal scientific semantic field, mentioning 'neural activity in the amygdala' (43). There is an allusion to the work of Paul Ekman, a twentieth-century psychologist. Ekman's scientific work on emotions is clearly of interest to Joe, who is trying to understand his 'apprehension' (43).

Joe is unsuccessful in taming his emotions and his behaviour reveals the paradox in his character. On the one hand, he is proud to be rational. On the other, one of his final acts in the chapter reveals his superstition. Bizarrely, Joe hopes for 'luck, or rather, protection' from metaphysical forces as a reward for replacing some marigolds back into the jam jar they have fallen out of (44).

The narrator's irrational fear is probably fuelled by the setting. He is in the exact spot 'where the policewoman, Yvonne Fletcher, had been shot dead by a Libyan' (44) during a protest outside the Libyan Embassy in 1984. She was in the wrong place at the wrong time and Joe is afraid that he too will suffer a similar fate. This **foreshadows** the restaurant gunman scene that occurs later in the novel.

CHAPTER 5

The first thing to note about chapter 5 is Joe's **unreliability** as a narrator. He makes himself 'a gin and tonic', so now his perception is affected by alcohol (46). Perhaps fuelled by drink, he makes up his mind that the man in the library was Jed and he decides to tell Clarissa about it.

Yet Joe is still wracked with doubt. He considers two possibilities: 'If Parry had been trailing me all day, then he knew where I lived. If he hadn't, then my mental state was very frail' (47). He admits his 'intuition' is unreliable, yet he is making decisions based on it, which would be characteristic of **Romantic** writers (47). Usually, Joe prides himself on his logic.

His next move is more rational. He dials 'last number recall' and hears Jed's answer-phone message (47). This confirms that Joe is probably being stalked by Jed. Joe even complements Jed's faith in a **metafictional** sense, mentioning how it reaches into the 'angles of his prose' (47).

Joe tries to escape his fear by immersing himself in his work. He uses a **tetracolon climax** to illustrate his scientific approach: 'Propose it, evince the evidence, consider the objections, re-assert in conclusion' , which he calls 'a narrative in itself' (48). He then mentions the nineteenth-century crossover between the arts and the sciences, when '[t]he dominant artistic form was the novel' (48). 'Downe House was more parsonage than laboratory', Joe says, indicating Darwin's pseudo-scientific, 'parsonical' narrative was affected by contemporary novels (48).

Joe continues with this digression from the plot and moves on chronologically to discuss scientific narratives in the twentieth century. Narratives were still of paramount importance and led to the quick acceptance of Albert 'Einstein's General Theory' in comparison with a more 'unattractive' theory propounded by Paul Dirac (49, 50). Joe describes Dirac's theory using the **semantic field** of music: '[I]t was a song sung out of tune' (50).

However, Joe is still uncertain, asking: 'What possible evidence could I produce to suggest that the novels of Dickens, Scott, Trollope, Thackeray etc. had ever influenced by a comma the presentation of a scientific idea?' (49). However, some eminent nineteenth-century scientists like Sir Richard Owen [who does not feature in *Enduring Love*, but was a contemporary of Darwin] were avid readers and there is plenty of historical evidence that show he was captivated by Charles Dickens, in particular. Perhaps, Joe is remiss when it comes to research due to his mental condition. He wavers again by the end of the paragraph, asserting that: 'It was though an army of white-coated Balzacs had stormed the university departments and labs' (50).

The allusion to Honoré de Balzac is yet another intertextual reference. There is a lot of **intertextuality** in the novel as a whole, but why Balzac is mentioned here is interesting. Balzac is considered to be one of the founding fathers of naturalism, which with its precise prose is diametrically opposed generically to **Romanticism**.

The **semantic field** of biology comes next, as Joe analyses his fear scientifically as 'Nerve terminals buried deep in the tissue of the heart secrete their noradrenalin' (51). He continues in this vein: 'More oxygen, more glucose, more energy, quicker thinking, stronger limbs' (51). It is a dramatic sentence, despite its scientific content. The absence of verbs ensures that it resonates on an emotional level.

What follows could be interpreted as a brief **shifting perspective**, as Joe says: 'Squirrels and thrushes can only look down on us and smile' (51). This is reminiscent of the 'buzzard' in chapter one (1). The bird's-eye view makes the action beneath seem insignificant and unimportant. It also could be a sign that despite his atheism, Joe believes in some kind of superior being(s) watching over him. It could just be a symptom of his paranoia.

His fears turn out to be unfounded as it is Clarissa who comes towards him 'rapidly across the room' (51). Here the plot fits comfortably into the generic conventions of a psychological thriller.

The chapter ends with a possible allusion to John Milton's *Paradise Lost*, as Joe interrupts his kisses with Clarissa to say: 'Before we go to Paradise' (53). An informal register predominates here, as Joe hypocritically condemns her brother, saying: 'He must be living inside a hard-on' just before making love to Clarissa (53).

CHAPTER 6

The first thing to note about chapter 6 is the **setting**: Maida
Vale. It is an affluent area of London, and despite its
waterside location next to the Regent's Canal the narrator's
assertion that 'something resembling the *Queen Mary* ran
aground' only confirms Joe's **unreliability** as a narrator (54).
However, the nautical metaphor cleverly conveys the
opulence of his and Clarissa's surroundings. The luxury-cruise
liner metaphor seems to be extended to describe the interior
of the apartment's floors as 'oak parquet' which 'could
accommodate any number of jazzy quick-stepping couples'
(54). This is very much in keeping with the popular image of
the *Titanic,* the ill-fated passenger liner that sank in the
Atlantic Ocean in 1912. According to some sources, the band
played on as the ship sunk and the last song was is widely
reported to be the Christian hymn: 'Nearer, My God, to thee'.
This image seems to be appropriate given Joe's affluence and
Jed's religion. However, although luxury-cruise liners from the
early twentieth century inevitably evoke such images, the
boat cited is the Queen Mary, not the Titanic. The narrator's
reliability is further in question due to his historical
inaccuracy. The Queen Mary was not launched until 1934, so
quite how 'something resembling' it ''ran aground in Maida
Vale' in 'the twenties' is a moot point.

Joe's mental state appears to be deteriorating, so can the
readers take his calculations seriously as he revisits the
balloon incident? Returning to the comforting **semantic field**
of mathematics, Joe calculates 'if we assumed an average

weight of a hundred and sixty pounds each, then surely eight hundred pounds would have kept us close to the ground' (55).

The narrative's semantic field moves into evolutionary psychology as Joe assumes the accident occurred because the scales tipped 'from altruism to self-interest' (55). This analysis relates to the work on Richard Dawkins, who wrote *The Selfish Gene* in 1976. He maintained that the more genetically related individuals are, the more likely they will be to act altruistically to each other.

After that departure into scientific and mathematical theories, Joe reflects on his own narratives, so this is an example of **metafiction**. He thinks of Jean Logan and an image comes to him 'from a half forgotten painting in the late Victorian narrative-style' (56). Joe is self-conscious about his writing and insecure: 'Narrative – my gut tightened at the word. What balls I had written the night before' (56). The sudden use of the **informal register** suggests that Joe's emotions are suppressing his analytical side.

Joe becomes more and more vulnerable, thereafter, which perhaps makes his character more sympathetic. When he tells Clarissa that Jed has said 'I love you' to him, her reaction is to giggle 'little-girl style' (57). Her character is childish as takes 'delight' in the revelation, saying: 'A secret gay love affair with a Jesus freak! I can't wait to tell your science friends' (57). Her 'levity' provides Joe with some 'comfort', according to the narrative. Yet as the discussion proceeds to Joe's assumption that Jed was watching him in the library, she is naturally skeptical about Joe's lack of evidence. Joe's frustrations seem to be coming to the boil, despite his claims about being comforted by Clarissa, when she replies: 'Don't get angry with me' (57). At the end of their conversation, Joe admits: 'I felt like a mental patient at the end of visiting hours' (58). Clearly, his mental state undermines his reliability as a narrator.

The juxtaposition of the 'visiting hours' sentence with the reappearance of Jed is interesting (58). It effectively **foreshadows** Jed's admittance to a mental institution at the end of the novel. However, it also builds tension, which is fitting for a **psychological thriller**.

Note the **syntax** at the end of the chapter. Short sentences are mixed with longer ones, as the reader gets a sense of the Joe's increasing anxiety as he hears Jed on the phone say: 'That's as promise. A solemn promise' (60).

Joe's narrative echoes Jed's last words: 'Solemn. More like panicky' (60). Despite the pressure he is under, Joe remains analytical, deciding Jed is 'pannicky' as opposed to 'solemn' (60). Joe slips back into the comforting semantic field of mathematics as he 'calculated: perhaps I should see him, let him see me and let him understand that I was distinct from the creature of his fantasy world. Let him speak' (60). The repetition of the word 'let' is interesting. It gives the final page of the chapter a church-like resonance, in the manner of a vicar speaking to his congregation, saying: 'Let us pray'.

CHAPTER 7

The first thing to note about chapter 7 is the **setting**: Jed is 'standing under a tree' (61). This echoes the opening of the novel when Joe and Clarissa are under 'a turkey oak' (1). The parallel ends there though, as this time the tree signifies menace as opposed to safety. There are the same Biblical connotations, however, linking the tree to the Tree of Knowledge. It almost seems as if Jed is guarding it. He is certainly reluctant to leave it. He could be regarded as the Biblical serpent that tempts Eve. However, in this narrative twist, the serpent is homosexual and he wants to honour the word of God rather than disregard it.

Joe seems to underestimate the threat posed by Jed, describing him as 'smaller, or knobs and bones' (61). Jed is wearing '[s]oft brown leather shoes, so it appears that Joe's narrative has been **unreliable** (62). 'No trainers today', Joe notes, almost as if he doubts his previous assumption that Jed was stalking him in the London Library (62). Joe still has a hunch that his previous assumption was correct, despite the glaring lack of evidence. So he asks Jed if he was 'following' him and interprets the absence of an answer 'as confirmation' (63, 64).

The characterisation of Jed is developed in this chapter. Joe notes that '[t]he whites of his eyes were exceptionally clear', which seems to indicate metaphorically that Jed sees himself as a religious visionary. The narrator also reveals Jed's 'conversational tic', which involves catching your eye before turning the head 'to speak as though addressing a presence at his side, or an invisible creature perched on his shoulder' (65). This shows Jed sees something more than Joe. Jed has seen the light of God.

Joe is unnerved by the encounter. 'It was if I had fallen through a crack in my own existence, down into another life, another set of sexual preferences, another past history and future' (67). It relates to the figurative Fall from Eden suggested by the balloon accident, and it also echoes Jed staring at 'a crack in the pavement' (62). It is almost as if Jed expects Joe to fall down that crack. It foreshadows Joe's later emotional state.

Yet Joe manages to control his feelings. He mentions 'how easy it was not to say, *Who the fuck are you? What are you talking about?*' (67). This shows how tolerant Joe is. As he puts it: 'I was playing along with this domestic drama, even though our household was no more than this turd-strewn pavement' (67). This is an example of **metafiction**, but rather than a novel's narrative, this is self-consciousness about a play's narrative. Theatrical **motifs** appear throughout the novel: for instance, the fifty-plus 'theatrical happy endings' that Joe witnesses at Heathrow (4).

Despite his admitting that he feels 'sorry for' Jed, whom he describes as a 'curious child', Joe makes his escapes in a taxi (67). Although he is not ostensibly threatening, Jed's suggestion that Joe and Clarissa 'meet this head-on' brings to mind head-on collisions or driving accidents (68). Given that Joe has already climbed into a motor vehicle, this figure of speech has a particularly relevant and threatening resonance.

It effectively means this chapter ends with a cliff hanger, for many readers will wonder if both Joe and Clarissa are in danger now. This plot device indicates this part of the novel, at least, falls into the generic category of **psychological thriller**. Also, Jed's understated **characterisation** makes the threat posed by him seem all the more real.

CHAPTER 8

The chapter begins with Joe recalling the events of the previous chapter and the confrontation with Jed, whom he always calls 'Parry' (69). The use of Jed's surname creates a sense of distance.

Joe further distances himself from the immediate action by thinking about his next writing job. He plunges himself into theories regarding biology and evolution. This theoretical digression helps dissipate the tension, so if the novel is to be judged as a psychological thriller, then its use is questionable.

However, this departure from the main narrative strand does add depth to Joe's character. The reader discovers that a few years ago, Clarissa had disparagingly referred to Joe as a rationalist 'gone berserk' or reductionist (70). This kind of insult has been thrown at the evolutionary scientist, Richard Dawkins, who claims most human behaviour is genetically motivated.

Reported speech is used to let the reader know about Clarissa's opinion, which is that 'the truth' of a baby's smile is 'in the eye and heart of the parent' (70). The use of reported speech makes the narrative appear scientific here. The formal tone is quite respectful towards Clarissa's point of view, as it remains objective.

The theoretical argument continues with Joe complaining that Clarissa is in love with the **Romantic** poet, John Keates. It is an emotional response to the situation.

However, Joe returns to the comfort of his scientific approach, maintaining the baby's smile is 'hard-wired' and present 'for good evolutionary reasons' (70). This discourse is academic and analytical, but Clarissa reminds Joe that 'synthesis' is 'crucial' (71). In other words, she wants him to open his mind to other forms of knowledge and to not be so reductionist.

McEwan uses **symbolism** to emphasise the sexual nature of Joe's next encounter with Jed. '[S]haved clumps of privet' could refer to trimmed pubic hair and Joe's keys could be regarded as phallic, especially when he says: 'I might slip the extended key right through him [Jed]' (72).

The tension rises in the scene as Joe enters his flat and calls the police. Quick, snappy dialogue follows with Joe appearing helpless and ridiculous. This episode seems to adversely affect his confidence. While Jed is sure of his purpose, Joe is wracked with self-doubt and is even cynical about his own professional skill as a scientific writer. Joe admits he has profited from 'swinging spider-monkey-style on the tallest trees' (75). Yet it could be argued that the Biblical Tree of Knowledge that Joe is metaphorically eating from, through his scientific writing, is the cause of his self-doubt. Ignorance is bliss, some say, but Joe is continually educating himself with evolutionary theories that challenge the idea of God.

The tree **motif** recurs, as does the 'dog' motif. Describing Jed with the simile, 'like a dog', the narrator subtly suggests that Parry's religious faith is similar (77).

Jed, meanwhile, sees symbolism in 'the curtains' (78). Symbolic language seems to be particularly important in this chapter, although the scientific discourse and the snappy dialogue with the police are also significant features of it.

CHAPTER 9

In this chapter, Joe tells the story from Clarissa's point of view. It is one the novel's famous **shifting perspectives**. It marks a **narrative transition** as we switch from a first-person narrative to a third-person one. Despite the shift in perspective, the reader still only sees the plot from Joe's restricted view of events. Therefore the narrative in this chapter is not completely **omniscient**.

Interestingly, Joe assumes a God-like position as editor of Clarissa's story. Given his atheism, Joe's stance could be considered somewhat ironic. Joe admits he 'construed' Clarissa's narrative but he does not explain how (79). This lack of explanation is particularly strange, bearing in mind that a lot of the narrative in previous chapters concerned itself with **metafiction**. As readers we have to guess how this has been constructed. Could it be from Clarissa's diary, her conversation, or a mixture of both? We know Joe is not afraid to pry and it is no coincidence that Clarissa's 'appointment diary' goes 'missing' (79).

The idea that Joe has used Clarissa's diary to construct the narrative in the chapter is borne out by the list of events that occur in it. These events appear to be random and unrelated to the other characters, so it subtracts from the suspense.

It is a disjointed account **syntactically**, as the tense switches from 'she arrives' into the past tense of 'the student she supervised yesterday' (79). Then the action slips back into more recent events, which once again arouse very little, if any, tension.

That changes when the next paragraph opens with 'she lugs her bags' (80). This time the tense remains in the present, giving Clarissa's needs a sense of urgency and immediacy. Using the **semantic field** of evolutionary science, she describes Joe as a 'newly discovered talking ape' (81). This is the kind of terminology that is more typical of Joe than Clarissa. He seems to have stamped his mark on her narrative as well as his own, and it could relate to his **unreliability** as a narrator. Clarissa continues to use the same semantic field, describing Jessica's Lowe's husband as a 'mate' in the biological sense (82).

As this is a **frame narrative**, it is difficult to discern which narrator is more unreliable, Joe or Clarissa. Ironically, she questions Joe's reliability and mental stability, when he claims there were thirty-three messages on the answer phone before he erased them. This could be an example of Joe's **hyperbole**.

Clarissa's **syntax** changes as she slips back into past tense to ask Joe about the police. The amount of dialogue increases as their dialogue reaches a crescendo and she says: 'Why did you wipe the messages off the tape?' (85). She believes that this 'throws him' (85).

She tries to get into Joe's head as she believes Joe's 'emotions are slow' and presumably underdeveloped (86). She claims that 'he has the wrong kind of intelligence' (86).

Her semantic field returns to what would be expected of an English lecturer, as she identifies the word 'even' as a 'reckless little intensifier' (86). In his frustration, Joe can only say 'Christ' in reply (86). This could indicate that he is turning to God.

Clarissa certainly has the upper hand; she feels a 'pulse of triumph' (87). The fact that Joe reports his inferiority to Clarissa, at this point, suggests that he is trying to maintain the neutral stance as editor of her narrative.

Joe's frayed mental state is soon displayed though when he tells Clarissa to 'fuck off' (88). Clarissa seems to be the innocent victim here, as she cannot possibly know that Joe 'wouldn't mind picking up the dressing room stool and throwing it' (88).

By the end of the chapter, it seems as if Joe cannot resist seeing things from his own point of view only. Perhaps emotion have taken him over. His rationality and logic has succumbed to a stronger force. It proves that Joe can be an unreliable narrator even from a third-person perspective.

CHAPTER 10

Here, the narrative returns to Joe's **first-person perspective**, shifting from Clarissa's point of view in the previous chapter. Joe's has just stormed out of his flat in the pouring rain, blaming Jed for 'coming between' him and Clarissa (89). Joe notices the 'sole' of his shoe has 'a long-neglected gash' (89). Perhaps, 'sole' is a **pun** for 'soul' for Joe feels his 'soul' is under attack, given Jed's relentless pursuit of it. Joe's lack of faith means his soul can be described as 'long-neglected'.

Joe is more worried about his 'fury' than his soul, and this is partly described in the **semantic field** of drama (89). He describes 'another thing too, like a skin, a soft shell around the meat of [his] anger, limiting it and so making it appear all the more theatrical'. He seems to feel trapped by the domestic drama he has just been part of inside his flat. Indeed, it is like a stage with Jed the only member of audience watching attentively outside. Joe realizes that 'curtain' is '[t]he key word', and somehow thinks this knowledge can help him (89). He visualises memories cinematically 'off the screen of recall' (89). He imagines 'a grand house' but admits 'if this was the house where the significant curtain hung, it meant nothing' to him (89, 90). By the time he feels 'for "curtain" again', there is 'no association at all, not even a shadow' (90). What the curtain means exactly is a mystery at this stage, but Joe realizes it is some way symbolic.

In fact, Joe's behaviour and language is suddenly much more in keeping with a **Romantic** poet than it is a scientific journalist. He seems to be experiencing an altered state of consciousness, almost like Samuel Taylor Coleridge's narrator in the poem 'Kubla Khan'. Joe even admits to indulging in a 'fantasy' that he 'was a poor down-and-out scurrying in the rain past the rich folks' houses' conveniently forgetting his 'own half-million-pound apartment' (90). He certainly seems to be unhinged.

Once his 'tormentor', Jed, catches up with him, Joe uses the semantic field of religion to express his desire for the demise of his pursuer: 'I never quite lost faith in the redeeming possibility of a bus crushing him as he stood there . . . pleading as he damned me' (91).

Joe describes Jed as 'a forlorn zoo bird' at this point (91). This **imagery** is appropriate given the caged nature of Jed's narrative, which is described as 'closed' by the critic Martin Randall (Peter Childs, *Ian McEwan's Enduring Love*, 59, Routledge: 2007). By that, Randall means Jed is not open to new information to change the course of his narrative as he has an unshakeable belief in God and love. Joe is completely opposite in this respect, being so wracked with doubt and having 'no idea where' he is 'going' (89).

In another respect, Jed is Joe's **Gothic** double. The narrative seems to acknowledge this by keeping the pair apart with 'a car surging up the middle of the road . . . with an angry blaring klaxon whose receding Doppler inverted his [Jed's] own sorry sound' (91). 'Doppler' appears to be a pun on the word 'doppelgänger', which is a paranormal double of someone.

Joe's mental faculties seem to be revived by Jed's 'extreme' condition and even more so 'by a word he [Jed] used twice: *signal*' (92). Now Joe tries to connects this word with his own sudden preoccupation and he reveals: 'I almost had it. A grand house, a famous residence in London, and the curtains in its windows used to communicate . . .' (92). The **ellipsis** at the end of the paragraph invite the reader to solve the puzzle before Joe. Although it is not the final paragraph, it leaves the reader with a mystery to think about, so works as a cliffhanger.

CHAPTER 11

Like chapter 9, chapter 11 contains a **frame narrative**. However, this time, it is more conventional as it is told from a **first-person perspective**, a bit like Victor's account to Captain Walton in Mary Shelley's *Frankenstein*. However, Jed's narrative is **epistolary**, like Walton's letters to his sister.

In *Enduring Love*, Jed seems to try to emulate Joe's writing style, using the **semantic field** of science when he writes: 'Dear Joe, I feel happiness running through me like an electrical current' (93). He describes 'the unspoken love' between them 'as strong as steel cable', extending the metaphor of electricity subtly to suggest it flows from one to the other in their relationship. It is interesting that the love is described as 'unspoken', a word often associated with **Gothic** novels.

Jed soon settles back into his more religious way of expressing himself and his description of Joe sounds uncannily like that of Jesus Christ carrying his own cross up a hill ahead of his crucifixion. Jed writes: ' Even now, when I bring to mind that moment when you started back up the hill and I remember the stoop of your shoulders, the heaviness in your stride that spoke of rejection, I groan at my behaviour' (94). Jed begs for Joe's forgiveness.

Jed goes on to list his personal history in the style of realist fiction and unifying this part with the rest of the novel is the **motif** of France. We find out later that the disease Jed is suffering from is de Clérambault's syndrome, named after the

French psychiatrist <u>Gaëtan Gatian de Clérambault</u> (233). At this point, Jed's mental problem is shrouded in mystery. However, the French connection is clear. He lives in Frognal Lane, which may relate to the French nation's appetite for frog's legs. He describes his house as 'a miniature version of some rather grand French place' (95). Jed adds more French details: 'It even has faded green louvred shutters and a cockerel weather-vane on the roof' (95). The word 'louvred' conjures up images of the Louvre in Paris, France, while the 'cokerel' is one of the national symbols of France.

Meanwhile, the very fact that Jed is 'writing' all this down brings Joe 'closer', for in a sense both are writers (95). In that way, Jed is Joe's **Gothic** double. Although, Jed is not a professional writer, he certainly has an eye for detailed beauty, describing the branch of a cherry tree growing 'through the railings' so he is 'close enough to see how the water forms into oval beads tinged by the flowers' pale pink' (96). The 'beads' that Jed mentions could be a reference to Catholic rosary beads, but that is a matter for conjecture for his exact religious denomination is not revealed.

The chapter ends with a paragraph in which Jed suggests that he join Joe and Clarissa to 'talk it through' (98). This is ominous reading for Joe, but it works well for the general reader as it adds to the tension and suspense, making it effective as a cliffhanger.

CHAPTER 12

Chapter 12 is a **frame narrative** of sorts, for Joe is journeying to Oxford, but goes back in time via **flashbacks** to his search through Clarissa's papers. Although Joe's mind reflects upon past events, his body is moving forwards towards Jean Logan's house, making it a **linear chronological** account of events. As readers, we learn about the narrative through Joe's **first-person perspective**.

Yet there are **other voices** in the chapter. A letter allows the reader to hear Joe's professor tell him to 'continue with the very successful career' he 'already has' (106). Joe is extremely disappointed to discover his 'proposal for work on the virtual proton' is now considered 'redundant'. This news is emasculating for Joe, who seems slightly feminized by his domestic **setting** until he takes to his car. He narrates: 'I lingered in the kitchen, clearing the plates' (101). This bears little resemblance to the more stereotypical macho hero that Joe tries to conform to in the first chapter, when he tried to save the boy in the balloon.

The double setting of the car and his flat gives the reader to discover two sides of Joe's character simultaneously in the same chapter. However, it is largely a reflective episode. The action is in Joe's mind. He admits: 'I was getting nowhere. For twenty-five minutes I sat in Headington High Street, waiting for my turn to pass the bus' (106). The first **short sentence** in the quote stands out and it is therefore dramatic. It is only a traffic jam but it highlights the fact that Joe is passive and helpless in his love life. The 'double-decker bus' that has 'broken down' and is blocking his way seems to be a metaphor for his relationship with Clarissa (106). From now on, metaphorically speaking, Joe could be about to continue his life as a single-decker bus.

Clarissa has exposed the introspective analytical nature of his 'inner double-entry book-keeping' and now it appears that they are on the verge of breaking up (103). Joe admits he is wrong via the semantic field of accounting: 'Balance, double entry. She was right' (103). Of course, the world of accounting is not a radical departure from mathematics, a field in which Joe is comfortable. So Joe is conceding a lot of ground to Clarissa in this chapter. He feels he has 'cruelly betrayed' her (101) and communication seems to have broken down, judging by the lack of **dialogue**. It is mostly reported speech in this chapter, and Clarissa's direct speech seems full of recriminations. For instance, when she says: 'His [Jed's] writing's rather like yours' (103). Consequently, Joe is full of self-doubt and wonders if his **love story** with her will continue. He asks himself a series of questions: 'Had she met someone? At work? A colleague? A student?' (104).

Joe even questions his own virility. He admits in a **measured educated** tone that: 'Self-consciousness is the destroyer of erotic joy' (102). He thinks Clarissa has 'misread' his 'expression' but wonders if he know what 'speaking from the heart' means (103). This links to his problem of accepting that emotions mediate rational thinking and behaviour. Yet as he reflects on how he opened Clarissa's private letters, Joe narrates: 'My rationalizations crystallised around a partial concept of justice' (105). He realizes that '[s]elf-persuasion was a concept much loved by evolutionary psychologists' but that does not prevent him from deluding himself (104). Joe believes that 'individuals' that behave in this way flourish (104). Jealousy has driven his actions: a pure emotion rather than the product of reason. Yet he tries to tie it in with his question about 'what was distorting Clarissa's responses to Parry' (105). This line of enquiry puts the chapter back into the genre of the **psychological thriller**.

Joe's failure to control his emotions makes him an **unreliable narrator**, as does his physical condition. Upon getting out of the car, Joe admits he 'may have entailed a slight reduction in blood supply' to his head (107). He admits: 'I didn't trust myself', so therefore it is also difficult for the reader to trust his perceptions too. He uses the metaphor of a 'stapler' to show 'how dishonestly we can hold things together' (107). By using the word, 'we', Joe seems to be including the reader. He is refusing to take full responsibility for his guilt.

CHAPTER 13

Firstly, let us look at the **narrative perspective and voices** contained in this chapter. Unlike some of the other chapters, one thing to note about chapter 13 Joe is less **self-conscious** as a **narrator**. McEwan simply tells the story, using a lot of **dialogue**, and does not analyse his own storytelling techniques. It seems he wants his readers to become more involved in the story at this point. However, we are still reminded about Joe's **unreliability** as a narrator, as he can't remember if the late John Logan left one or two car doors open. Joe replies to Jean's question: 'Two. I'm not absolutely sure, but I think two' (113).

Secondly, let us consider the **setting**. The talking takes place in Jean Logan's home. Although she goes to the kitchen, Joe remains in the sitting room, '[f]acing the poisonous fire' (110). He cannot be sure that the gas appliance is leaking toxic fumes, so this description is hyperbolic. Maybe it is a metaphor for his position regarding Jean. She is full of poison now that he husband is dead and she will exude plenty of hot air in the forthcoming scene.

While he is alone, Joe browses through Jean's book collection. This gives McEwan to make some subtle allusions to Victorian writers. The narrative mentions the work of four historians: Thomas Babington Macaulay (1800-1859), Thomas Carlyle (1795-1881), Edward Gibbon (1737-1794), George Macaulay Trevelyan (1876-1962); and one art critic: John Ruskin (1819-1900). As well as indicating that Jean teaches 'history at the University', it also suggests there is no future as Joe does not mention any modern books in Jean's house (110). The place seems tinged with death, as even the plants are 'sprays of dried twigs' (109). It is spartan accommodation with 'no comfort' (108). As Joe mentions **self-consciously**, 'it seemed a perfect setting for sorrow' (109).

The sorrow is the dominant emotion in what can be regarded as Jean's **love story** with John. Although, it is only a sub-plot, her suspicions of her late husband mirror Joe's, which he has already manifested by going through Clarissa's papers in chapter 12. Jean interrogates Joe like a policeman, and in that sense the **form** of the novel in this chapter conforms to the genre of the **detective story** or **crime novel**. Jed barely gets a mention in this chapter, so on a superficial level it does not feel as much like a **psychological thriller** as before. Joe tries to mention Jed's name, saying: 'There was my friend Clarissa, two farm labourers, a man called . . .' (113). Jean cuts him off in mid-sentence. It could be argued this adds to the tension because Jed is suddenly unmentionable, yet the terror he potential still lurks in the shadows of Joe's mind.

Jean's sorrow is so raw and real that Joe finds it difficult to think of other things during this scene. Without significant flashbacks, the **structure** then is **chronologically linear**, apart from Joe's brief recollection of 'visits' he 'had made over the years to various professors of science' (108). There is not much movement in the scene at all. Jean makes him tea, questions him and then presents him with 'a heavily weighted white carrier bag' (115). She sees this as evidence of her late husband's infidelity. It is interesting that the bag is described this way, as her questions to Joe could be regarded as 'heavily weighted' also. Therefore, 'weighted' may be a pun.

In terms of **language**, there is a lot of detail when it comes to description. Joe describes the similarities between himself and Jean using the semantic field of chemistry: 'What I saw in Jean's grief reduced my own situation to uncomplicated elements, to a periodic table of simple good sense: when it's gone you'll know what a gift love was' (112). This is a good example of **measured, educated language** and yet it ends in a traditionally **romantic** style. Also, there is something Romantic with a capital 'R' about his description of Jean , looking like 'a lone Arctic explorer' (108). The metaphor is extended as Joe mentions 'a brown igloo-style tent' (122).

However, Joe's descriptions are largely in the background as Jean dominates the scene through the use of **dialogue**. Joe has little time for reflection, apart from the aforementioned **intertextual references** to Victorian writers, as jealous Jean is firing the **questions** at him: 'There was someone with my husband. Did you notice?' (113). Her **short sentences** get straight to the point. She tries to find out the truth 'in the tone of an aggressive barrister' (114). The violent language continues as she threatens to 'kill' her late husband's alleged lover, just as her two children enter the room at the end of the scene (117).

CHAPTER 14

The past tense of the verb in the opening sentence that begins: 'It was with a touch of sadness' marks the chapter out as a **retrospective** account (118). The word 'sadness' sets the mood, which the reader can predict will be melancholy. Joe adds that Clarissa told him: 'I would have made a wonderful father' (118). The modal verb 'would' works in the same way here, making it an especially sad moment from a **first-person perspective**. Joe will not be able to be the biological father to Clarissa's children. The idea of him being a 'wonderful father' is **ironic** and particularly distressing to Joe, who seems to subscribe to the theories expounded by Richard Dawkins in the *Selfish Gene* (1976). Likewise, first-person narratives can be seen as selfishly skewed, as all events are seen through the eyes of an active participant in the plot. Therefore, bias and prejudice are likely, despite Joe's attempts to narrate in the neutral tones of scientific discourse.

However, the reader hears **other voices** in the chapter via direct speech and **dialogue**. Leo is the first to speak when he says: 'It's completely wrong to kill people' (119). A moral debate ensues as Joe explains 'moral relativism' to the children (120). Rather than using that academic term, Joe uses an anecdote to explain the concept to Leo and Rachael. He says: 'When I was in Morocco I was told that I should never pat children on the head' (120).

Joe saves his **measured and educated language** for his own reflections. He explains: 'I saw myself configured in their [the children's] eyes' (119). He seems to be reacting very emotionally, despite his scientific language. For instance, when he imagines that Leo and Rachael regard him as an 'aged' and 'large man in a creased blue linen suit, the coin of baldness on his crown visible from where they stood' (119). This is an example of shifting perspectives, and Joe's attention to unflattering details makes him appear self-conscious about his own appearance. This is ironic, given he is a self-conscious narrator with a penchant for metafiction. While Joe may have guessed the children's viewpoint correctly, he is, in fact, jumping to conclusions. Joe is mirroring Jean's behaviour in the previous chapter; she, of course, mistakenly believes her late husband has had an affair. Jean has misread the situation, the way that Jed misreads what he interprets as **signals**, elsewhere in the novel.

Curtains are particularly symbolic to Jed, and it is interesting that this **motif** makes a reappearance without him in this chapter. The narrator tells us: 'Leo squealed from behind the long curtains that framed the french windows' (121). We later discover that 'Leo had wound himself up in the curtain' before telling his mother: 'But this is our palace and I'm the king and she's the queen and I only come out when she gives the signal' (123). Leo's speech jogs Joe's memory, when he suddenly remembers: 'The palace was Buckingham Palace, the king was **King George Fifth**, and the woman outside was French, and the time was shortly after the Great War.' Although there is a **time reference** in this sentence, this is not a flashback at all. The action of the **linear** narrative continues **chronologically** with nearly all the action taking place in Jean's sitting room. The **setting** only alters when Joe gets into his car and prepares to wave goodbye to the Logan family, only to discover that 'all three had gone back inside the house (125).

Returning to Joe's **introspective narrative** for a moment, he regards the French woman's obsession as a 'forlorn and embittered love' (124). It is unrequited and 'her affair with the King' is simply a figment of her imagination (123). Although, Jed is not compared directly, the similarity is obvious: 'He [The King] used the curtains in the windows of Buckingham Palace to communicate with her' (124). Then Joe remembers the name of the 'French psychiatrist [. . .] who gave his name to her morbid passion. **De Clérambault**' (124).

Joe's slow revelation adds tension to the plot. The implied similarity between the fictional Jed and George V's real-life stalker makes the danger that Joe is facing seem all the more real. This exposition works well in the genre of the **psychological thriller**. However, it is a **love story** too, as the French woman 'knew for certain [. . .] that the King loved her. She loved him in return [. . .]' (124). The novel's hybrid nature is further complicated by it also being a **detective story**, with Jean using certain clues to imagine the details of her late husband's alleged affair: 'He was showing off to a girl' (123). She uses emotive language to add that they are 'all suffering for it now' (123). That assertion is not strictly true as, soon afterwards, Leo is 'flushed and happy' while Rachael starts 'to giggle' (123).

However, Jean is so convinced that she is correct about her recreation of events surrounding her husband's death that she is loath to ask Joe **questions** about what actually happened. Her lack of questions contrasts with Joe, who seems less certain in this chapter. He uses a lot of questions in his interaction with Jean's children. He asks Leo: 'Have you ever heard someone say "I'm so hungry I could eat a horse"?' (119). Joe really knows the answer to his question, so he is really using language to play teacher to Jean's children.

CHAPTER 15

Looking at chapter 15, the **narrative perspective** is obviously in the **first person retrospective** as, from the start, it begins: "On the way home I turned south of the motorway" (126). The word "turned" shows the narrator is speaking in the past tense and, of course, the word "I" indicates that he is also speaking in the first person.

Apart from Joe, there are two other **narrative voices** within this chapter. On his way back to his apartment, Joe encounters Jed. The dialogue that follows includes **short sentences**, which speed up the pace of the narrative in the dialogue. Jed says to Joe: "Did you get my letter?" (129). This reminds the reader of the epistolary nature of Jed's previous narrative involvement. However in this chapter, Jed is expressing himself through direct speech.

In stark contrast to Jed, Clarissa's direct speech is wordier. She says to Joe: "I thought this would be the first place you'd look" (132). Then she adds: "Didn't you think I'd be going through your desk while you were out? Isn't that how it is with us these days?" (132). In fact, it is Clarissa's voice that ends the chapter with a question: "What is it you're trying to tell me?" (132).

Looking at the **setting** for a moment, Joe moves off the motorway into the field where the balloon accident took place. The "nettle patch" that Joe describes hints at his atheism, for it is there "where Parry had wanted to pray" (127). This hilly setting is described by Joe theatrically as "the stage". Later, Joe parks outside his apartment, goes inside, then into his kitchen, and finally finds Clarissa in his study. He describes the sounds he hears in their flat. Joe says: "Buildings have their own sound archives of creaks and clicks, mostly prompted by small changes in temperature". Notice he uses the **language of science** to make himself feel less distressed. Yet Joe is still illogical when he admits "I had simply misread the air" (131). But we will cover the **use of language** in the chapter a bit later.

The **form** in chapter 15 is generically that of a **psychological thriller**. In particular, the use of tension adds to the suspense. For instance, when he considers the threat that Jed poses to his life, Joe reveals that: "[I]f a researcher was easy to hire, so too were a few goons to thrash me within an inch of my life" (130-1). He admits he could be "over-interpreting" (131). If this is so, then it is another example of the unreliable narrator being foregrounded. The phrase, "something was wrong", works effectively in the genre of the psychological thriller because the reader is left to consider various chilling possibilities (131). The plot also conforms to the genre of a **love story**, at the end, when Joe encounters Clarissa. Their confrontation in Joe's study is typical of a lovers' tiff in a more romantic genre.

There is a **linear chronology** in chapter 15 with only occasional and briefest of **flashbacks**. For instance, when Joe walks 'to the point' where he met Jed and saw John Logan 'fall from the sky' (127). There is a lot of movement in this chapter and some dialogue too, but the action scenes are mostly focused on the present. However, once again, Joe - the

unreliable narrator - is foregrounded when he imagines **de Clérambault** "in a double-breasted suit" (128).

There is a certain amount of **measured educated language** in this chapter. For instance, when Joe discusses de Clérambault's syndrome, he describes it as "a dark, distorting mirror that reflected and paraded a brighter world of lovers whose reckless abandon to their cause was sane" (128). This kind of language is more **ornate** and more in the style of **literary romance** then we are accustomed to expecting from Joe. The language is **emotive** as he describes de Clérambault as being like "a bridegroom at the altar" for giving his name to the "pathological love" that Jed is suffering from (128). This kind of imagery is in keeping with a stereotypical love story. Joe even imagines the car that Jean Logan was asking him questions about in the previous chapter. Now Joe imagines that "the front doors had stood wide open, like wings" (128). There is something almost angelic and, therefore, **religious** in this description.

Earlier in the chapter, there is the **use of modal verbs** to create an alternative storyline. Joe imagines what might have happened to the mystery woman mentioned by Jean Logan in the previous chapter. Joe says: "Standing by the passenger door she would have had a clear view of the whole drama, from the balloon and its basket dragging across the field, to the struggle with the ropes, and the fall. She wouldn't have been able to see where he landed" (126). Joe then further speculates: "Or she might have gone the other way, down the hill towards Watlington" (126).

There is also the **use of detail**, particularly in regard to Jed. Joe describes Jed is almost like a negative photograph. This is very much in keeping with the idea that Jed is Joe's Gothic double. Joe describes him in a "black suit, white shirt buttoned to the top, black painted shoes with white flashes" (128). Later, Joe mentions Jed's eyes, which to him appear "smaller" (129). This makes Jed seem more menacing. Joe also refers to Jed's "shaving cut", which seems to foreshadow the self-inflicted violence which is to come later in the novel (129).

CHAPTER 16

Looking at chapter 16, the words "dear Joe" indicate that the form is epistemological. Through a letter written by Jed, the reader finds out his point of view in this **frame narrative**. The perspective has shifted from Joe to Jed yet the **narrative perspective** is still the **first person retrospective**. The next words that Joe writes show that to be the case: "the student I hired rang my bell".

The **setting** is also revealed in this opening sentence the reader discovers that the time is 4 PM yesterday (133). The same is Jed's house, but movement takes place as he meets the student he hired at his "gate" (133). Jed then retires to what his "mother used to call the library" (133). Jed's description of the room with "bare" shelves indicates that he lacks learning (133).

The setting changes briefly as Jed flashes back to the past. In his first brief **flashback**, "in the early morning", Jed mentions "the taxi" that he took in order to come to Joe's apartment (136). His second flashback is a little longer. Jed writes: "I remember I once went walking with my school in Switzerland in the summer holidays. One day we spent the whole morning climbing a boring rocky path. We all complained-it was so hot and pointless, but the teacher made us keep going" (137). This long winded description is similar to a religious sermon. Despite that Jed's poor education, he is still capable of vividly describing scenery, for example: "just before lunch we arrived onto a high Alpine Meadow, as huge sunny expense of flowers and grasses, with electric green mosses around the banks of the stream" (137). Jed claims that someone from his school described the place as "Paradise" (137). However it appears to be Jed's view and therefore the reader can assume that this narration is as unreliable at least as Joe's.

Although the form is epistemological, generically it still conforms to what readers expect of a **psychological thriller**. The threat that Jed poses is very real when he writes: "you were asleep, unaware of your own vulnerability, indifferent to the protection you enjoy from a source whose existence you deny" (134). Jed makes it seem as if only God is protecting Joe from harm. Further threats follow, when Jed writes: "my love to you is hard and fierce, it won't take no for an answer, and it's moving steadily towards you, coming to claim you and deliver you" (136). Once again, Jed is characteristically using the semantic field of religion. Words like "deliver" suggest as much.

Surprisingly, Jed's **language** becomes quite **scientific** at times as he tries to get into Joe's head. Jed writes: "my brain was like a washing machine – churning and spinning, full of your dirty washing" (137). It is interesting that Jed describes the green mosses of Switzerland as "electric", as has already been discussed. He seems quite adept at describing the world scientifically, despite claiming he "was never much good at school" (135). He summarises Joe's work by writing "little mineral pools warmed by the sun, chemical bonding, protein chains, amino acids etc. The primal soup" (135). He then explains to Joe that "describing how the soup is made isn't the same as knowing why it's made, or who the chef is" (135).

This is typical of the argument that religion has had with science.

At this point in the narrative, Jed has already used three **rhetorical questions** to get Joe to rethink his scientific rational philosophy. Jed writes: "who cares about the carbon dating of the Turin Shroud? Do you think people changed their minds about their beliefs when they heard that it was a mediaeval hoax? Do you think faith could depend upon a length of rotting cloth? (134).

Jed is also unintentionally ironic when he claims that he must set Joe "free from his little cage of reason" (133). Already at the beginning of the chapter the reader has seen Jed being handed a bundle of articles "through the bars" (133). It appears that Jed is he one incarcerated by his mind rather than Joe.

It is also ironic that he considers Joe to be a child, describing his books and articles as "the little footstampings of a tired infant" (136). Already Jed's hyperbolic language in this chapter has marksed him out as a bigger child than Joe. He describes the time he spent reading Joe's articles as "the worst few hours" of his life (133). This kind of exaggeration is childish.

Finally, the chapter closes with Jed threatening Joe, telling him: "never try to pretend to yourself that I do not exist" (138). Jed seems to be confusing himself with God. They both have three letter names, as does Joe.

CHAPTER 17

The first thing to note about chapter 17, is that the **narrative perspective** is in the **first person**. Joe begins the narrative as follows: 'I don't know what led to it' (139). The word 'I' indicates that the narrative is in the first person, while the word 'led' shows it to be a retrospective account. Joe's narrative is also **self-conscious**, as he proves when he analyses his own writing: 'I wrote a long and dull review of five books on consciousness. When I started out in science-writing the word was more or less proscribed in scientific discourse' (139-40). Thereafter, in his next metafictional study, Joe analyses Jed's letters: 'They were generally long and ardent, and written in an increasing focused present tense' (141). This subtly indicates that the threat posed by Jed is coming closer. Joe's narrative is also **unreliable** as he cannot be trusted to tell the truth, admitting, albeit hyperbolically, that: 'every word [he says to Clarissa] is a lie' (140).

Other **voices** figure in the chapter. Firstly, there is Clarissa saying: 'Joe, it's all over' (145). This conforms to the stereotypical **love story** genre. Then, more in keeping with a detective novel, Joe makes phone calls to find out more about the events surrounding John Logan's death and the mystery person in his car. Toby Greene's mother tells Joe to 'bugger off' (146), which echoes what Joe pretended he said to Jed in a previous chapter. Although, it was a lie technically, it was simply a watered-down version of what he actually, which was: 'fuck off'.

Eventually, Joe speaks to Toby, but the reader only hears the latter say: 'We've been to the benefits people three times now . . .' (146). Not much is revealed, as Joe edits the rest of the conversation out of his narrative.

He then speaks to James Gadd's wife, who appears to be middle class, judging by her response to Joe's request: 'I'll have a jolly good try'.

Finally, he gets though to Joseph Lacey, who says: 'Sleeping dogs, I'd say' (147). This is an unintentional pun, as it seems to refer indirectly to Jed, who is sometimes compared to a dog. Of course, Lacey is really referring to the idiom: 'Let sleeping dogs lie', in which the awake metaphorical dog is more dangerous than the one that lies asleep. This idiom works effectively in the genre of the **psychological thriller**, as it inadvertently increases the tension. When Lacey says: 'I'm not talking about it on the phone', the suspense increases another notch, as the reader anticipates a meeting leading to a revelation (147).

The **setting** does not change much in this chapter. It begins in Joe and Clarissa's bedroom and ends there, although the latter announces at the end: 'I'm going to sleep in the children's room tonight' (149). This is **ironic**, seeing as they have no offspring of their own. The time is 'between half past one and two in the morning' and they are 'lying in bed' (140). Only 'the low light of lamp' illuminates the room. In the semi-darkness, Joe can reflect **introspectively** on his situation.

He uses the **language of science**, not unexpectedly, perhaps because he finds mental security there. Although he initially uses the language of a typical love story, explaining: 'We were loveless' (140), Joe reverts to his more characteristic style. He now compares his love life to 'Harrison's Fourth Sea Clock', which he maintains is 'anachronistic to recreate' (140). It is true, as Rupert T. Gould found out when he tried to reconstruct John Harrison's marine chronometer. The reconstruction required oil to work and, as it degrades each time it is used, it is now out of service. This metaphor effectively describes their relationship, which needs lubricant to continue and is inevitably dwindling away.

Joe's **measured educated** tone continues as he describes the threat posed by Jed, in almost nuclear warfare terms: 'they'd be warning' (144). He describes his relationship with Clarissa similarly, using the semantic field of the army when he narrates: 'We were immobilised' (139).

His references to **literary terminology** is less expected. He narrates: 'I thought I heard the shuffling iambs of her pulse in my pillow' (144). He is struggling to controls his emotions and just before has contradicted himself, by referring to his own 'logical heart' (144). As well as being an **oxymoro**n, it seems to show Joe's instability.

The reader is also exposed to the **language of entrapment** as Joe refers to 'love's prison', when he considers Jed's situation. As far as Joe is concerned, Jed is 'crouched in a cell of his own devising, teasing out meanings, imbuing nonexistent exchanges with their drama of hope or disappointment' (143).

Structurally, the chapter progresses with a simple **linear chronology**. Only generic **flashback**s take place as Joe catalogues 'routine' events that take place now that Jed is in his life (142). One episode seems to reveal that Joe is teasing Jed, as he admits: 'I lingered by the privet and ran my hands along it to imprint it with a message, and then I turned his way and looked at him' (143). Joe seems almost coquettish, at this point.

CHAPTER 18

Early on in chapter 18, the reader can see that the **narrative perspective** is in the **first person**. The second sentence is as follows: "when I gave her a card she kissed me full on the lips" (150). The word "I" shows that the narrative is in the first person, and the word "gave" is "give" in the past tense so therefore it is a **retrospective** account.

Other **voices** also make their way into the narrative. The reader hears Jed's voice via a letter, which is quoted in the narrative. Jed sounds threatening as he enjoys the "power of death "(151). He adds that he loved "the little thing" that he had "just destroyed" (151). Jed's menacing tone works well within the context of the **psychological thriller** genre.

A third voice is heard later in the chapter, so the reader gets access to the direct-speech patterns of "Duty Inspector" Linley (154). Linley uses short **questions** to interrogate Joe. Some questions are so short that they only consist of one word, for instance: "Obscenities?" (155). This quickens the pace of the narrative. However, his speech becomes more bureaucratic as the chapter progresses. For instance, when Linley says: "There's nothing here that is threatening, abusive or insulting as defined by Section Five of the Public Order Act" (157). These longer sentences show the mechanism of bureaucracy stifling Joe's complaint.

Moving on to language, for a moment, it is interesting that Joe also uses the **semantic field of administration** to express himself in this chapter. No more so than when he gathers "all

Parry's letters together", arranges "them chronologically" and fixes them "in a clasp folder" (150). Joe continues in this vein, but is **self-consciously** aware of the language he is using, hoping to get "the administrator's illusion that all sorrow in the world can be brought to heel with touch-typing, a decent laser printer and a box of paper clips" (151). He mistakenly believes that the "cumulative effect" of his compilation of "a dossier of threats" will "not be lost on the mind of a policeman" (151).

This kind of language prepares the reader for what lies in store for Joe in the police station. Using **pathetic fallacy**, McEwan illustrates the ineffectiveness of the police. Joe describes his surroundings in the interview room, as follows: "the ashtray was the sawn-off butt of a plastic Coke bottle. Near it squatted used teabag on a spoon" (154). The word "squatted" is not exactly a dramatic action verb. In fact, it indicates the opposite, that not only the police but everything around them is useless. There is even a suggestion of corruption, when Linley tells "the lads in puffer jackets" that if they both leave immediately the "might see" his "way to losing that file" (158).

The fourth voice that appears in this chapter is that of Clarissa. Although she mimics a "know-all radio voice", it appears that she could be copying Joe (161). In answer to Joe's question about whether or not he is "some kind of evolutionary throw forward", Clarissa answers that: "evolutionary change, speciation, is an event that can only be known in retrospect" (161). Clarissa appears to be using Joe's language to express herself and, to a point, ridicule Joe.

Perhaps Joe is trying to do the same, using the basic poetic technique of alliteration, when he describes his girlfriend as: "Clarissa the Keats scholar was crouching naked on a cork stool" (161). Or perhaps Joe is displaying his admiration for Clarissa. He admits that for his allegations against Jed to be taken seriously, he would need "the skill of a literary critic like Clarissa to read between the lines of protesting love" (151). Unfortunately for him, Clarissa is not on his side in this respect, but nonetheless this may be Joe's tribute to her skills.

The narrative structure's **linear chronology** begins on Wednesday in this chapter, which is a significant milestone in their relationship being "Clarissa's birthday" (150). Structurally, the narrative then progresses to when Joe leaves "the flat in the late morning" only to "sit for over an hour in the waiting room" of the police station (153). The setting that awaits Joe in the police station, as already mentioned, is challenging. Joe narrates: "Linley waved me into one of two metal stacking chairs. We faced each other across the Formica table patterned in coffee rings. At every point on its surface my cold chair was greasy to the touch" (154). The reader begins to feel that Joe is in an uncomfortable and unfriendly environment, and therefore can truly understand his frustration with the bureaucracy that he encounters.

The delay at the police station causes Joe to be "late for lunch" as he makes his way "up the street, away from the station" looking for a taxi (158). As he hurries "along the Harrow Road", the narrative setting flashes back to the "early morning" of Clarissa's previous birthday (158-9) . However, rather than describing details of the setting, Joe mostly recalls the script of "a radio talk" that he was "going to record that afternoon" (159).

Then Joe remembers "the night before" Clarissa's birthday one year ago, and begins to explain in **educated, measured** tones and how "sexual" functions operate alongside higher functions, such as "memory, emotion, fantasy" (160). Joe concludes that "all copulating creatures are vulnerable to attack, but selection over time must have proved that reproductive success was best served by undivided attention" (161). This extended, **introspective flashback** reminds Joe "how sharply" he "missed" their "old life together" (161). The setting then returns to the present time, as "a taxi" approaches (161).

The birthday setting enhances this chapter's credentials as a love story. For instance, when Joe gives her a card she kisses him "for on the lips" (150). Yet within the same paragraph, Joe reveals that his research indicates that "Parry's condition could not stand still" (150). This means the threat that Jed poses is growing and therefore is very much in keeping with the genre of the psychological thriller.

However, the form is predominantly that of the **love story**, as even the when Joe discusses Jed's letters, he uses terms that fit into the love-story format. For example, when he narrates that: "after an hour or so I realised it was a mistake to concentrate on over expressions of frustration and disappointment – that I had started it all that I was leading on, teasing him with false promises, reneging on my undertakings to live with him" (151).

Although it is a love story, the threat that Jed poses puts this chapter firmly in the realms of the psychological thriller also. For instance, when Jed rights to Joe, "I went to Mile End Road yesterday – you know, where the real villains live. Looking for more decorators!" (152). The word "decorators" is a euphemism for murderers or assassins. The understated nature of Jed's language makes the threat that he poses all the more menacing.

Jed's religion verges on the demented, as for him: "God was a term interchangeable with self" (152). Through his letters, Jed even makes references to the biblical story of Job. In the Bible, this didactic poem shows the relationship between love and pain. Ominously, Jed writes: "We are both suffering, Joe, we are both afflicted. The question is, which one of us is Job?" (153).

CHAPTER 19

At the very opening of chapter 19, it is obvious that the narrative is **retrospectively** in the **first person**, as Joe narrates: "I arrived twenty minutes late" (162). The use of the past tense of "arrive" shows the retrospective nature of the account that follows. The use of the word "I" shows the narrative is in the first person.

The **unreliable** nature of the narrator is revealed soon afterwards. Quite early in the chapter, Joe asks himself whether he would remember "the conversation now" if he "did not know what it proceeded?" (163). This demonstrates that Joe wonders about his own reliability as a narrator. He admits that he cannot "remember what food we ordered after" the antipasto "was cleared away" [164]. Joe realises that traumatised memories cannot be trusted.

He claims that he resisted the temptation to rewrite this account, when he narrates that: "a day or so later it became a temptation to invent or elaborate details about the table next to ours, to force memory to deliver what was never captured, but I did see the man, Colin Tapp, put his hand on his father's arm as he spoke, reassuring him, soothing him. It also became difficult to disentangle what I discovered later from what I sensed at the time" (166).

However, Joe offers an incredibly **detailed** description of the restaurant which provides the **setting** for the attempt on his life. He describes the place **geometrically**, narrating that: "the ice bucket sat within a rhombus of sunlight on a white table-cloth, the tall restaurant windows showed off rectangles of blue sky between the buildings" (162). He has already informed us that it is "lunchtime", so the readers have a clear idea of the time setting (162). When Joe steps into the restaurant the "conversation was at a roar and stepping in from the street was like walking into a storm" (162). The readers can very easily imagine the level of sound in this description of the setting. They can also imagine the colours evoked by the food. As Joe narrates: "In memory, all the food they brought us first was red: the bresaola, the fat tongues of roasted peppers laid on goat's cheese, the radicchio, the white china bowl of radish coronets" (163). The red and white colours are reminiscent of Jed's allegedly entrance into the library in a previous chapter and foreshadows the attempted murder. The colours recur at the end of the chapter when Joe narrates that: "The silenced bullet struck through his [Tapp's] white shirt at his shoulder and lifted him from his chair and smacked him against the wall. The high velocity impact forced a fine spray, a blood mist, across our table-cloth, our deserts, our hands, our sight" (172).

The bungled assassination attempt ends the chapter, which has progressed **structurally** in a **linear chronology**. All the events has have taken place during lunchtime, apart from the intertextual and historical references. Professor Jocelyn Kale relates the story of "Phobos Levine at the Rockefeller Institute" which has startling parallels with Jed Parry (165). In the **frame narrative**, Phobos dismissed certain findings regarding DNA because "it became a matter of faith with him, deep faith" (165). Jocelyn dominates the **dialogue** with his scientific knowledge.

As well as hearing Jocelyn speak via direct speech, the reader also gets to hear Clarissa quote Keats. However, much of Clarissa's digression on Keats is via Joe's reported speech.

The only other voice the reader hears is Jed's "dog-like yelp" (172). Although, Joe "failed to recognise" Jed, the dog analogy means the reader can be more certain that it is him.

The attempted murder makes the **form** of this chapter rather like a **crime novel**. However, Professor Jocelyn's digression into the world of science makes the chapter more like a **scientific treatise**. Then, of course, there is the ongoing **love story** between Joe and Clarissa, as he mentions: "before I sat down I kissed. These days our tongues never touched, but this time they did" (162).

Still in keeping with the genre of the love story, Joe quotes what he **self-consciously** describes as "the chocolate box lines" to Clarissa before giving her a present. He says "beauty is truth, truth beauty . . .' (166). This echoes something Joe has narrated about Albert Einstein in a previous chapter. It also echoes the words of Jocelyn who says: "you know what poor Rosalind [Franklin] said when they showed her the model they built of the DNA molecule? She said it was simply too beautiful not be true . . ." (165).

Joe's language slips into the **semantic field of booksellers**, thereafter when he describes Clarissa's gift: "Foolscap octavo in drab boards with back label. Condition, poor, foxed, slight water damage. A first edition of his first collection, *but Poems* of 1817" (166).

There is also the **intertextual** reference to William Golding's *Lord of the Flies*, and how it was initially rejected by publishers (171). Prior to that, Joe reveals that years ago at a party he had "gone down on drunken these to get her [Clarissa] to recite from memory 'La Belle Dame Sans Merci' (169). This is similar to the story of Haydon asking Keats "to repeat the ode to Pan from *Endymion*" in front of Wordsworth (168).

Pathetic fallacy also appears within this chapter. As already mentioned "the tall restaurant windows showed off rectangles blue sky", suggesting that the windows themselves are fashionistas! Likewise, the table where Joe sits in the restaurant has human qualities, metaphorically. When the masked intruders are noticed, even Joe's "table was staring shamelessly" (171). Of course, the word "table" is usually taken to mean all the people eating at the table, however it could still be an example of pathetic fallacy and, consequently, it adds to the shocking nature of what is happening.

The guilt of the would-be assassins is revealed by the "priestly look" and "ceremony in the stillness". The **semantic field of religion** warns the readers that Jed is responsible for this mayhem.

CHAPTER 20

The **narrative perspective** here is the **first person** as we find out in the first sentence, when Joe reveals: "I sat in the police station" (174). The word "I" reveals that the narrative is in the first person; and the word "sat" is the past tense of the verb "sit" and therefore means the narrative is being retrospectively told.

As would be expected in a chapter that features **dialogue**, there are a number of **voices** in it. But before that the reader experiences the newspaper headlines following the attack in the restaurant. Joe reveals these headlines to the reader. As would be expected, the newspapers use **hyperbole** to report what happened, for instance: "restaurant outrage", "lunchtime nightmare" and "bloodbath" (174).

We also hear the voice of Clarissa, when she receives Joe's gift. She gratefully says: "It's a wonderful present", but then she warns Joe not to "go on about" his "usual stuff" (175). This comment from Clarissa suggests that Joe is an **unreliable narrator** who is mentally unstable.

Detective Constable Wallace is the next to add his voice to the narrative. In a typical policeman style he sets about taking a report from Joe, who considers the officer and the process to be "pedantic" and steered "towards irrelevancies" (176). Initially, the reader only hears Wallace begin the interview with the following words: "OK. Let's go from the beginning" (176). Wallace begins taking notes and after he's finished he reads it back to Joe. When Joe hears the account being read back to him he admits: "it was a prose I immediately wanted to disown" (176). Once again, Joe is becoming **self-conscious** about his narrative skills. He interrupts Wallace saying: "Sorry. That's not what I said" (176). The reader is left to wonder whether or not Wallace has correctly taken down Joe's story. The other possibility is that Joe is so distraught after what happened that he cannot remember what he has just told the officer.

The setting in chapter 20 is interesting in that this police station is located in "Bow Street" (174). This brings to mind the Bow Street Runners, who were London's first police force back in 1749. This police force was set up by Henry Fielding (1707-1754), who was an eminent writer of fiction. Perhaps this location was intentional on the part of McEwan, who may be trying to show that Joe is becoming more literarily sensitive. The time reference allows the reader to know that: "it was only a few hours on and already we were headlines in the evening paper" (174). Clearly, Joe Clarissa and Jocelyn are in the police station waiting room in the late afternoon. By the time Joe gets home by taxi, it is "already dark" (182). The reader can picture Joe in the street, checking the "side streets", looking behind the "privet hedge", and "round the side of the building" for signs of Jed.

After that, Joe listens in the lobby and mentions the music he hears from a nearby flat, which he attributes to "Anton Bruckner", who was one of the leading lights of Austro German Romanticism in the 19th century (183). The reader receives a blow-by-blow account of how Joe goes up the stairs, and lets himself in before going into the kitchen and see and Clarissa's note. Interestingly, Joe dissects the note looking for signals very much in the way the reader would expect Jed to. Clarissa's note reads: "Dead tired. Talk to you in the morning, Love, Clarissa" (183). Joe is so sensitive, at this point, that he looks at the word "love" and wonders if the uppercase "L" means anything. He then goes from "room to room, turning on lamps and securing the windows", before entering his study (183). He settles on the "chaise longue" and goes through one of his address books, which he calls his 'Domesday Book' (183). This is an example of **intertextuality** within this chapter.

Moving on to **language** for a moment, there is a proliferation of French words throughout the novel. Later, we hear the voice of Stendhal fire Clarissa's teachings. Joe accurately remembers the French words: "Le mauvais gout mène aux crimes" (185). This roughly translates as "bad taste leads to crime". This kind of language clearly means the chapter is veering into the territory of the **detective novel**. Incidentally, Marie-Henri Stendhal (1783-1842) was a realist writer, and so the previous French quote is yet another literary allusion.

Although Joe has allowed himself time for **introspection**, he is still nervous about his surroundings. He listens in the "semi-dark of the hallway" but only hears "the creek and click of contracting wood and metal, and, deep in the pipework, the trickle of retreating water" (188). The narrative paints a soundscape for the reader in this chapter, with Joe even noticing the sounds from the kitchen and "the soothing rumble of the night-time city" (188). Joe returns to his study to take decisive action. That action is to call Johnny B. Well, who provides another voice in the chapter.

As already mentioned, Joe analyses Clarissa's note in the kitchen. The fact that he does this suggests that the form of the narrative is a **love story**. It is, of course, also a crime novel hence the involvement of the aforementioned Bow Street police. However, one of Joe's comments to Wallace firmly puts the chapter into the realm of the **psychological thriller** genre. He tells the detective constable: "There's a man out there who wants to kill me" (176). The reader can sense the fear in Joe and now that there has been a shooting in the restaurant it seems the threat is more than a figment of his imagination. The terror experienced by the main protagonist is increasing and that is typical of a psychological thriller.

Structurally, the narrative progresses in a **linear chronological** fashion. Only Joe's digressions take the reader away from the present. For instance, he mentions: "a friend who had been wrongly diagnosed with a terminal illness" (177). Using the metaphor of a drowning swimmer, and a **modal verb**, Joe suggests one possible fate for his friend: "the waters would close over her head" (177). Joe then compares his situation in the police station, narrating: "It was not quite self-pity, though there was an element of that, more a kind of shrinking into one score, shrinking so deeply that everything else – the veritable tourists, the stricken girl – appeared as though on the underside of a thick glass panel. As I returned to the waiting room, my thoughts swam randomly in their little aquarium" (177-8). It now appears that Joe sees himself, metaphorically as a floundering human in a fish tank.

As well as expressing himself metaphorically, Joe cannot resist using the **semantic field of mathematics** in his narration. When Joe describes how he, Clarissa and Jocelyn waiting to be interviewed, he comments: "statisticians call this kind of thing random clustering" (174). He continues in this vein, narrating: "We lived in a mist of half-shared, unreliable perception, and our sense data came warped by a prism of desire and belief, which tilted our memories too" (180). Apart from showing Joe's penchant for using mathematical terms like "prism", it also shows his own unreliability as a narrator. Joe tries to justify this in **evolutionary scientific** terms, suggesting: "We're descended from the indignant, passionate tellers of half truths who in order to convince others, simultaneously convinced themselves" (181). This is just as well as his powers of recollection of failing him. When Wallace repeats the question: "What flavour was the ice cream?" Joe can only reply incorrectly that the flavour was "apple" (181). In fact, Joe first narrated that the flavour was "lime" and the ice cream was in fact "sorbet" (171). The word "apple" could have **religious connotations**, if we see it as the fruit taken from the Tree of Knowledge in the biblical story in Genesis.

Predictably, Joe retreats into the world of science where he feels more comfortable under interrogation. He narrates: "Neuroscientists report the subject is asked to recall a scene while under a magnetic resonance imaging scanner show intense activity in the visual cortex, but what a sorry picture memory offers, barely a shadow, barely in the realm of site, the echo of whisper" (182). Joe is clearly distressed as the long sentence seems to indicate. He seems to feel his brain cannot do justice to the true images that he saw, and he likens it to looking at "blurred daguerreotypes" (182). As well as being from the semantic field of photography, this is yet another reference to something French.

CHAPTER 21

In chapter 21, the reader quickly finds out the **setting** and the **narrative perspective** as the opening sentence begins: "The next morning I drove Johnny out to a house on the North Downs" (189). Of course, the word "I" indicates that the narrative is in the first person and the word "drove" shows that it is a **retrospective** account. Meanwhile, the time setting is "the next morning" after Joe's phone call to Johnny.

There are a number of **voices** in this chapter, and the first we hear is Johnny's. An informal register is expected from a drug dealer and, in this respect, Johnny does not disappoint when he says: "It's like in banks. You never say money. Or in funeral parlours, no one says dead. With guns no one ever says gun. Only pricks who watch TV say shooter or piece. If you can, you avoid naming it at all. Otherwise it's the item, or the wherewithal or the necessary" (189). There is a **humorous** quality about Johnny setting up a ridiculous protocol regarding **euphemisms**.

The next voice that the reader encounters is that of Steve. Like Johnny, he is quite ridiculous in terms of appearance, and perhaps his initial utterance upon opening his front door is a little clichéd when he says: "Johnny B. Well!" (192). Steve seems rather stupid as he does not even know which day of the week it is. Steve insists that it is "Friday" (192). Johnny, meanwhile, is only one day out with his belief that it is: "Saturday" (192). Joe corrects them by telling them that it is: "Sunday" (193). Despite everything that Johnny has forbidden Joe to say, Steve breaks Johnny's protocol by simply asking

Joe if he is: "the guy who wants to buy a gun and bullets" (193).

The reader next hears the voice of Daisy who says: "We are having a late breakfast. We've had to start again" (194). The breakfast setting is more like "the Mad Hatter's tea party", according to Joe (195). This makes Joe regard Steve as "the dormouse" in Lewis Carroll's novel, and this description is a literary allusion to the hippy's doziness.

Meanwhile, Daisy appears to be a believer in astrology. For instance, she uses the **semantic field of fortune-telling** when she says: "there is an overriding monetary aspect with particular reference to the signs and the tenth house" (197). This appears to be a house where New Age beliefs rule the roost, judging by Xan's declaration that: "Everything is connected, we know that now, it's been shown, it's a society. It's basically holistic" (199).

To some extent, the characters in this house could be viewed as **caricatures**. On that very subject it is interesting that the small town of "Abinger" is referred to in the chapter (191). Of course, the eminent novelist and essayist E.M. Forster is connected with that place because of a book he wrote entitled: *Abinger Harvest* (1936). However, Forster is more famous for writing: *Aspects of the Novel* (1927). It is in the latter book that Forster discusses the difference between flat and round characters in novels. Interestingly, McEwan's new characters that appear in this chapter are arguably flat. That point of view is reinforced by the fact that Xan has a verbal tic. He continually says the word "basically" (196). This makes his character easily identifiable in the dialogue that follows. Joe is very critical of Xan's use of "percentages snatched from the air, the unprovenanced research, the measurements of the immeasurable". This would particularly irk someone with the scientific and mathematical ability of Joe.

Finally, we hear the voice of Jed on the phone. He simply says: "Joe, is that you?" (203). He then, **structurally**, ends the chapter on a **cliffhanger** by adding: "I make your place, sitting here with Clarissa. I'm putting her on, OK? Are you there? Joe? Are you there?" (203). The reader can only wonder what has happened to Joe. Has he fainted? Is he in a state of shock? If so, what will he do? All these answers are expected in the following chapters.

Continuing on the subject of structure, the **linear chronology** of this chapter is largely unaffected by digression. This makes the pace of the narrative more relentless than is the case in other chapters. The **dialogue** and the fight between Steve and Xan also have a similar effect.

From a language point of view, Joe uses the fight to make a **scientific allusion** to "a gestalt candlestick", which measures cognitive performance (201). This is ironic as both Steve and Xan seem to have limited mental faculties. Joe also uses the metaphor of "a burst balloon" to describe "the crack of" Xan's hand on Steve's face. This reminds the reader of the accident which took place in chapter 1.

There is also the **literary allusion** to Bertrand Russell (1872-1970), who was a founder of analytic philosophy. Joe has similar beliefs to Russell, who has been described as an antagonistic atheist. Johnny describes the hippies as "intellectuals" and adds that: "they think they're Bertrand Russell was something. You will probably hate them" (190). It is a little surprising that Joe introspectively decides: "I already did" (190). In a sense, this is **ironic** given Joe's beliefs, which seem to be held by the hippies also.

In describing them, Joe uses the **semantic field of sailing**. For instance, he describes Daisy's "long straight hair" as "a last rope to the bollard of her youth" (194). Shortly afterwards, Joe describes Steve's moustache as "the pointy masts of the schooner I built as a kid" (195).

Inevitably, the **language of weaponry** exists in this chapter and it allows Steve to show some expertise when he says: "It's a Stoller .32, made before the factory was sold by the Norwegians back to the Dutch and German conglomerate that developed it originally. It's got a carbide twin-action release" (198). Perhaps Steve is not as stupid as the otherwise seems. Nevertheless, Joe has little respect for him and describes him in naval terms as: "human meaning appeared to be deserting the sinking ship of the face" (195).

Despite the pace of the narrative in this chapter, the words: "Time slowed" show its inherent **self-consciousness**. However, there is no lessening of the tension as shortly afterwards Joe tells the hippies: "I'll tell you in for words and nothing more. Someone wants to kill me" (199).

This puts the chapter firmly in the genre of the **psychological thriller**, especially when the **dog motif** is added to the equation. Of course, Jed has been compared to a dog in previous chapters, so each time the dog is seen or heard it is a reminder of the never decreasing danger presented by Jed. For instance, when Joe is under pressure and "they were all looking at" him they hear "the mongrel whine" through "the open french windows" (199). The french windows are particularly effective here as Jed is suffering from an illness named after the Frenchman, de Clérambault.

CHAPTER 22

A student's response to an exam question about McEwan's narrative techniques in chapter 22.

McEwan tells some of the story in chapter 22 through characterisation. The reader sees Jed's character develop right through until the chapter's climactic end.

In chapter 22, the reader witnesses more of Jed's aggression than has been previously been the case. In preceding chapters, Jed is comparatively calm and collected, albeit prone to emotional outbursts. To get Joe's attention, Jed has now become much more aggressive.

Jed poses a real threat now. The reader learns that Jed 'pulled out a short-bladed knife' and 'he brought the tapering point of the blade right up under his own ear lobe'. This action shows how dangerous and mentally unstable Jed has become, as he is prepared to mutilate himself just to get attention from Joe. The cutting of the ear could be an historical reference to the artist Vincent van Gogh, who cut off his ear to prove his love. Similarly, Jed wants to prove his love for Joe, but his actions only provide the reader with more evidence of his mental illness: de Clérambault's syndrome. The extremely terrifying nature of Jed's actions in chapter 22 make this scene an effective climax in the novel's narrative structure.

Another way in which Jed tells the story is through destination. McEwan creates the destination by using tension to show where the narrative is heading. 'I had the impression of having passed out for a second or two. The roar in my ears, I realized, was the car's engine'. The idea of Joe being virtually half-asleep while driving creates tension as the reader wonders whether or not Joe will be able to reach the climactic ending. The tension of the previous chapters culminates in chapter 22. There is a sense of Joe racing against time, which is a traditional narrative device to keep the readers on tenterhooks. Jed's line: 'It's all down to you, Joe' shows that the denouement may be approaching.

*Mark – AO2: Band 4 (*To score higher, look carefully at how **structure, form and language** affect **meaning**.)

The first thing to note about chapter 22 is the **first person retrospective narrative perspective**: 'I had the impression' (204). The word 'had' is in the past tense and 'I' denotes the narrative is in the first person. The narrative is **linear, chronologically** and **time-compressed**, somewhat **self-consciously** given the proliferation to time references.

Before the wounding of Jed, the time references seem to add to the dramatic tension. Joe tells Clarissa it is going to take him 'a couple of hours' to get home, so the reader must wait too for the expected rescue attempt (204). A little later, Joe uses a **simile** to compare Clarissa to 'a speaking clock' (204). Of course, as a hostage, Clarissa cannot be herself, but nonetheless it is a very unusual way to describe a character who has been representing emotions, amongst other things, throughout the novel. And with the hostage plot playing itself out here, it seems to be falling into the **psychological thriller** genre.

As well as a proliferation of time references, looking at syntax reveals a lot of **dramatic action verbs**, which you might expect given the **climactic** nature of the chapter. For instance, 'I shifted from second to fourth' shows Joe physically moving his gearstick. More dramatic action verbs follow as Joe talks about the gun secreted in a shoe box: 'I lifted it up and aimed it' (205). He adds: 'I turned the gun over' (205).

Interestingly, there is a distinct lack of action verbs in the climactic shooting scene, when Joe says: 'I aimed at his right side' (213). Joe does not say he pulled the trigger. It is almost as if he wants to be completely blameless.

The number of **voices** speaking short lines in the early part of the chapter add suspense and pace as the reader hears Joe, Jed, Clarissa and Johnny speak, respectively.

Next, the chapter slips into the **semantic field** of guns, as Johnny explains to Joe: 'It's a ten-shot'. Words like 'catch', 'stock', 'magazine', 'safety lever' and 'Browning nine millimetre' show that Johnny is experienced when it comes to guns. In direct contrast, Joe is inexperienced and the lack of technical language used in the narrative when he shoots Jed emphasises that.

The difference between Joe and Johnny, despite the similarity of their names, is clearly demarcated when Joe begins to use the lexical field of evolutionary science, 'drawn from game theory', to analyse his situation (206). He mentions that 'for any social animal, always cheating was a sure route to extinction' (206). This, of course, relates to the novel's theme of altruism, while Joe's reflections also slow down the pace of the narrative.

It quickens again in the same paragraph, as Joe uses **modal verbs**, which show the rising tension. Joe admits: 'I knew I shouldn't be wasting time. I should be racing towards London' (206). More modal verbs follow to illustrate Joe's increasing pessimism about his chances of successfully rescuing Clarissa. Using modal verbs, he sets up an alternative outcome: 'Fine – if I could find someone to dispatch an elite squad to abseil in on Parry and overpower him before he could do harm. What I'd get though, if I was lucky to reach their level with a phone call, would be Linley or Wallace, or some other weary bureaucrat' (208).

Later in the chapter, I think McEwan teases the reader with fake **foreshadowing**. For when Joe narrates: 'I prefer the earthbound scale of the biological', the reference to the earth could be taken to symbolically mean impending death (206-207). Later in the chapter, a near fatality rather than a death occurs.

McEwan's self-conscious style comes the fore as he explains in **metafictional** terms that the 'narrative compression of storytelling, especially in the movies, beguiles us with happy endings into forgetting that sustained stress is corrosive of feeling' (213). This partly explains why Clarissa has become relatively emotionless and physically cold towards Joe.

Each of the three protagonists seems to have altered his or her philosophical stance. Roles have almost been reversed.

Clarissa has become more rational, judging by the aforementioned simile likening her to a speaking clock and her reaction to being rescued by Joe. Meanwhile, Jed has shown his more artistic side, by threatening to cut his own ear off van Gogh-style with his 'blade' (212). Finally, Joe - the rationalist - seems to have given up on his philosophical stance somewhat when he tells the reader: 'In a world in which logic was the engine of feeling, this should have been the moment' when Clarissa and he can be intimate (213). Joe adds: 'such logic would have been inhuman', which suggests that he can no longer be accused of being a reductionist (213). His character has been transformed and now he recognizes that emotions interact with logic to produce patterns of human behaviour.

As well as his philosophy, Joe 's **syntax** also alters during this chapter, for instance when he relates what he has been charged with by the police: 'Possession of an Illicit Firearm, and Malicious Wounding with Intent' (214). As well as using the semantic field of crime and the capitalization typical of a police report, the absence of a verb in the syntax could indicate Joe's lack of guilty feelings.

He continues to narrate without verbs in this **setting**, which is the third scene in this chapter: 'My third visit to a police station in twenty-four hours, the third in my life' (214). The syntax is different in each of the three **settings**: Joe's car being the place for a profusion of dramatic action verbs, while his apartment produces the opposite effect on the narrator's syntax. Actually doing something about the intruder is much more difficult than indulging in 'a daydream of taking a shot at him' (209).

One final thought on chapter 22. I have read somewhere that it contains a **denouement**. Personally, I cannot see that at all. No loose ends are tied up at the end of it. The reader does not know if Joe and Clarissa will stay together or not when Joe says: 'Perhaps we really were finished' (215). As well as being a **cliffhanger**, this sentence also makes the narrative appear to belong in the genre of a **love story**.

I would describe the shooting of Jed as the novel's **climax**. What immediately follows is **falling action**, but not a denouement. Many novels are written in this format: exposition, rising action, climax, falling action and denouement; on the face of it, *Enduring Love* seems to follow that blueprint.

CHAPTER 23

Chapter 23 is a little bit different from the norm because it is a **frame narrative**. The form is **epistemological** due to the fact that the chapter is composed of one single letter from Clarissa to Joe.

Clarissa's letter begins: "Dear Joe, I'm sorry about our row" (216). There is a similarity between this chapter and chapter 11, which also begins in the **present tense** with "Dear Joe, I feel happiness running through me like an electrical current. I close my eyes and see you as you were last night in the rain" (93). Likewise, Clarissa's letter to Joe discusses the previous night. She writes "I hated it last night" (216). Ironically, Clarissa's letter is far more negative than Jed's, which refers to "joy"(93). However, they are both similar in as much as they are written in the first person with a mixture of present and past tense, the latter making it a **retrospective** account.

Clarissa's letter uses **repetition** for effect, for instance when she says "shoulder to shoulder", it fits into the **semantic field of the Army**. It seems to be a direct quote from Joe, so he is the additional voice in the narrative. Meanwhile, this choice of **language** makes their **love story** appear to be almost like warfare. However, Clarissa is offering Joe an olive branch because she also repeats "I'm sorry, really sorry" (216).

Clarissa continues in the vein of the love story by writing: "You forgot to take me along with you, you forgot how to confide" (217). The tone of her letter is quite accusatory. However, Clarissa admits she was wrong, and owes Joe "a profound apology for not standing" with him, for doubting his "sanity, and not having faith in" his "powers of rationality and deduction and" his "dedicated research into" Jed's "condition" (216). This is ironic, bearing in mind Jed's deluded yet strong faith has caused some many problems for the couple.

Some of Clarissa's writing delves into the **semantic field of counselling**. For example, she asks Joe: "isn't it possible that Parry presented you with an escape from your guilt? You seem to be carrying your agitation over into this new situation, running your anxieties with your hands over your ears, when you should have been turning on yourself those powers of rational analysis takes pride in" (217).

As far as the **setting** is concerned, most of the action mentioned in this letter happened in the flat that she shares with Joe. For instance, she writes: "That same evening you stormed out of the flat, slamming the door on me" (217). The door, in this case, is a **metaphor** for Joe's feelings. Clarissa feels that Joe has locked her out of his heart. She questions Joe's state of mind, writing: "I don't want to go on about it, you're ransacking my desk was a terrible betrayal. What reason and I given you to be jealous?" (217).

Although Clarissa wants to focus on the love story aspect in her letter, the **psychological thriller** genre comes to the foreground when she mentions Jed. She writes: "I don't accept that it was always inevitable that Parry was going to hire killers or that I should end up being threatened with a knife" (218). Clarissa is still trying to play down the threat that

Jed presented. She explains: "My guess was that he was always more likely to do himself harm" (218). Despite her claim that she will "always be grateful", it appears that she attaches some blame to Joe for what has happened (218).

Clarissa is a highly educated person, yet she questions whether or not de Clérambault's syndrome is "really" a "disease" (218). On a pedantic level, she is correct for the syndrome is usually described as a deluded condition.

She ends by writing: "I always thought I love was the kind that was meant to go on and on. Perhaps it will. I just don't know" (219). This relates to the idea that the title *Enduring Love* could mean a love that goes on and on. By a cruel twist of fate, it appears that it will not. At this stage in the novel, the title is **ironic** as far as Clarissa's love story with Joe is concerned.

CHAPTER 24

This chapter returns to Joe's narration. The opening sentence: "Ten days after the shooting I drove to Watlington" shows the narrative is in the **first person retrospective** (220). The word "I" shows is in the first person, and the past tense of drive, which is "drove" proves it is a retrospective account.

From this opening sentence the reader can also gauge the time **setting:** "Ten days after the shooting" (220). Eleven days after the shooting, the reader finds Joe in his "study making arrangements on the phone" (220). Once again, Joe is planning a picnic with wine. This shows the cyclical nature of the novel, as at the beginning Joe was "kneeling on the grass with a corkscrew" (1). However, this time the wine is Italian, as opposed to French. Perhaps Joe has had enough of French products, since discovering his stalker is suffering from a French-sounding psychiatric problem. Joe even seems quite superstitious, calling Clarissa a "familiar" (221). Usually, a witch's familiar is a spirit or animal that the witch can trust.

Ironically, Joe reveals there is very little familiar about Clarissa. He notes: "the print dress was new, and so were the green espadrilles. Even her skin looked different, paler, smoother" (221). The espadrilles gives her image a sense of Spain and, as Joe notes, she is "transforming herself into a separate person" (221). Nevertheless, Joe also uses the **semantic field of evolutionary science** to describe Clarissa as his "mate" (221).

As Joe becomes increasingly insecure, he retreats into his customary **educated measured** tone and even suggests that Clarissa is "thinking of the centrifugal geography – Maida Vale and Camden Town, Miami and Tokyo – that was whirling our lives apart" (221-2). Clarissa appears to be determined to keep the **love story** going, poignantly asking Joe: "What's the point? It's beautiful here and we're still unhappy" (222).

In response, Joe becomes increasingly **introspective** and admits that he "dreaded more personal talk in such an enclosed space" (222). The enclosed space that Joe is referring to is his car. Joe mentions that Clarissa is staring "through the windscreen at the road rolling under our feet and, to the left and right, the thickening films in the cow parsley just out along the hedgerows" (222). This is the beautiful scene that Clarissa was referring to. Given her love of **Romantic** writing this should be the perfect setting for her to rekindle her love with Joe.

Suddenly, via a **flashback** of sorts, Joe returns to his "sitting room in a state of dream-like agitation" (222). He cannot recover from what he describes as "Parry's legacy – an orgy of mutual accusation, an autopsy that sent us weary embittered to a separate beds at three in the morning" (222). Once again he returns to **nautical imagery** to express his feelings about Clarissa's letter: "Here was a diseased consciousness clamouring to batten itself to mine" (222). It is ironic that Joe calls Clarissa's consciousness "diseased" when Jed is the one who is incarcerated. It is also ironic that Joe uses the term "orgy" to describe their sexless lives together. The bitterness is almost tangible.

The **idiom** that Clarissa used in her letter, "shoulder to shoulder" is used by Joe in this chapter as he narrates: "Now here we were in six feet of space, shoulder to shoulder in fact that the matter of our differences was unbroachable" (223). Despite the tension inside the car, the environment outside seems relaxing. For instance, Joe describes: "The trees lining the tranquil street made a tunnel of green light broken by brilliant points of sunshine" (223). This setting appears to be idyllic.

Apart from the occasional flashback, the **structure** of this chapter is that of a **linear chronology**. The narrative moves briskly on as Joe and Clarissa arrive at the Logans' house. It is here that the reader hears other **voices**, such as Leo, who opens the door to say: "I'm not a tiger, I'm wolf" (223). This comment seems to indicate that Joe and Clarissa have lost their animal side of their relationship and now only behave "like a married couple invited to lunch" (223).

The reader then hears the sunbathing Rachael calling out to Clarissa, who is tickling her with a stalk: "I know just who you are, so don't think you can make me laugh!" (223). Like Leo, who is "naked but for face paint", Rachel is also in a state of undress "working at a tan" (223). This is another reminder of Joe and Clarissa's lack of physical intimacy.

Although the **form** so far in the chapter has been that of the love story between Joe and Clarissa, some mystery enters into the narrative, as Jean Logan says "I know I've asked to hear this, but I'm not sure I can go through with it, especially with Rachael and Leo here" (224). The reader may wonder what exactly is going to happen and this part appears more in keeping with the genre of the **detective novel**   .

The reader discovers another narrative voice, when James Reid explains his perspective of the balloon incident to Jean Logan. He says: "you're living through this tragedy, this terrible loss, and heaven knows, the last thing you need is this extra pain. The scarf left behind in your husband's car was Bonnie's" (227). This information is misleading and causes Jean to interrupt. But Reid goes on to explain further: "Bonnie and I are in love. Thirty years between us, all very foolish, but there it is, we are in love" (228). This love story parallels Joe and Clarissa's, in a way, as Reid echoes echoes Clarissa's apology in her letter to Joe, saying: "I'm deeply, deeply sorry" (229).

The meadow becomes foregrounded in Joe's consciousness at this stage, and he mentions: "the golden swathes of buttercups, a pack of horses and ponies galloping towards the village at the far end, the distant drone of the ring road, and close by, on the river, a sailing boat race proceeding with silent intensity" (230). Once again we have nautical imagery, and perhaps the relaxing qualities of water are what Joe needs after his harrowing experiences.

One voice the reader expects to hear within this chapter is that of Bonnie Deedes. As her surname suggests, perhaps her actions speak louder than her words, as we don't hear a single utterance from the young lover of Reid. She is conspicuous by her absence from the **dialogue** and Joe concludes: "she was even then – a genuine dumb blonde – or contemptuous of us all" (230).

THE APPENDICES

Appendix 1

This psychiatric report is written in the **third person** in a neutral, objective style. The layout of this appendix is extremely **authentic**. However, the letters of the names of the authors "Wenn" and "Camia" form an **anagram** for Ian McEwan.

The subtitle of the report begins without a verb, which is not surprising and then it goes on to class the syndrome as a "nosological entity" (223). This means what Jed is suffering from is being classified as a disease. Of course, Clarissa has doubted that the syndrome could be classed as such in a previous chapter. Now she is being proven wrong.

Using a **flashback**, the report explains the history of de Clérambault's syndrome, beginning in 1942. It then uses flashback again, to go back to 1918 when "a 53-year-old French woman" thought that "King George V was in love with her" (234). Even in the report, the genre of the **love story** still exists.

The **semantic field of** the report is that of **mental health**, which is not unexpected given that it is supposed to be taken from the British Review of Psychiatry. One example of this are the words: "the diagnostic criteria for the primary syndrome" (235). The report goes on to quote other medical experts, such as "Enoch & Trethowan", "Mullen and Pathe cite Perez", French psychiatrist Jean-Etienne "Esquirol", "Bucknell and Tuke", and "Lovett Doust & Chistie" (235 & 240). It is almost as if the sheer number of **voices** adds weight to the authority of the scientific judgment.

The report considers the case history of "P". While it is common practice to keep the patient's anonymity, it also incorporates the language of the criminal justice system as it mentions that Jed "was referred from the courts following charges arising out of the attempted murder" (236). The prognosis for Jed is pessimistic, as he appears to be suffering from "a most lasting form of love, often terminated only by the death of the patient" (242). Again this relates to the genre of the love story. In stark contrast, the report reveals that "in this case R [Joe Rose] and M [Clarissa Mellon] were reconciled and later successfully adopted a child" (242). The latter pair's enduring love has had a happy ending.

It's worth mentioning, that despite the report's neutral tone in general , Jed's voice still appears in the narrative, as he is quoted saying "on God's glory" and "bring him to God" (237). This suggests that Joe is not altogether safe from Jed's threat yet. However, the reader discovers that Jed "should be held indefinitely at a secure mental institution" (238). If that is so, the novel at this point ceases to be a **psychological thriller**.

Through the report, the reader can see the whole plot unravel from a more neutral perspective. However, if the reader discovers or notices that the report is a **fake** it lessens its impact on the reader's emotions. It is difficult to discover though, for even the references are painstakingly researched and the document seems to be very authentic.

Appendix 2

This letter from Jed to Joe is written in the **first person retrospective**. Jed writes: "Dear Joe, I was awake at dawn" (244). The word "I" indicates that the letter is written in the first person, and the word "awake" shows the narrative is in the past tense and therefore retrospective.

We have already found out in the previous appendix that Jed "gained entrance to university", joined the "Student Christian Movement", and "left university with a poor degree in history" (236). He even trained to become "a teacher of English to foreigners" (236). This shows that Jed has a level of education that he tends to play down, perhaps Joe's benefit.

In this **epistolary structure**, Jed uses **alliteration** to express himself: "the twigs at the very top are tangled against the sky, like the inside of some machine with wires" (244). Couched within that literary language is the word "machine", which is often connected with science and therefore Joe. Jed follows up that sentence with another praising "the resplendence is of God's glory and love" (244). It is interesting that he is counting his letters, almost like Joe - the mathematician - would, as Jed reveals he has just written his "thousandth letter" to Joe.

We find out from the words above the letter that this is written "towards the end of" Jed's "third year after admittance" (244). The exact time **setting** is something of a mystery, as Jed only reveals that it is "Tuesday" (244). He also reveals he woke "at dawn" to watch the sunrise (244). This is very much in keeping with the idea that he is a **Romantic writer**.

Jed continues to pile on the literary devices, using **ascending tricolons** to express his emotions more fully. For instance he tells Joe: "I adore you. I live you. I love you. Thank you for loving me, thank you for accepting me, thank you for recognising what I'm doing for our love" (245). He signs off with three words: "faith is joy" (245). It appears he will be relentless in his pursuit of Joe, who will never be completely safe. Therefore it continues to be a **psychological thriller** even after the last page is turned.

Useful information/Glossary

Allegory: extended metaphor, like the grim reaper representing death, e.g. Scrooge symbolizing capitalism.

Alliteration: same consonant sound repeating, e.g. 'She sells sea shells'.

Allusion: reference to another text/person/place/event.

Ascending tricolon: sentence with three parts, each increasing in power, e.g. 'ringing, drumming, shouting'.

Assonance: same vowel sounds repeating, e.g. 'Oh no, won't Joe go?'

Bathos: abrupt change from sublime to ridiculous for humorous effect.

Compressed time: when the narrative is fast-forwarding through the action.

Descending tricolon: sentence with three parts, each decreasing in power, e.g. 'shouting, talking, whispering'.

Denouement: tying up loose ends, the resolution.

Diction: choice of words/vocabulary.

Dilated time: opposite compressed time, here the narrative is in slow motion.

Direct address: second person narrative, predominantly using the personal pronoun 'you' in the narrative.

Dramatic action verb: manifests itself in physical action, e.g. I punched him in the face.

Dramatic irony: audience knows something that the character is unaware of.

Ellipsis: leaving out part of the story and allowing the reader to fill in the narrative gap.

Epistolary: letter/correspondence-driven narrative.

Flashback/Analepsis: going back in time to the past, interrupting the chronological sequence.

Flashforward/Prolepsis: going forward in time to the future, interrupting the chronological sequence.

Foreshadowing/Adumbrating: suggestion of plot developments that will occur later in the narrative.

Frame narrative: narrative within a narrative.

Gothic: another strand of Romanticism, typically with a wild setting, a sensitive heroine, an older man with a 'piercing gaze', discontinuous structure, doppelgangers, guilt and the 'unspeakable' (according to Eve Kosofsky Sedgwick).

Hyperbole: exaggeration for effect.

Intertextuality: links to other literary texts.

Irony: amusing or cruel reversal of expected outcome or words meaning the opposite to their literal meaning.

Metafiction/Romantic irony: self-conscious exposure of the devices used to create 'the truth' within a work of fiction.

Motif: recurring image use of language or idea that connects the narrative together and creates a theme or mood, e.g. 'green light' in *The Great Gatsby*.

Novel: 'a piece of prose fiction of a reasonable length' (Terry Eagleton, *The English Novel: An Introduction*).

Omniscient narrative: all-seeing third person narrative.

Oxymoron: contradictory terms combined, e.g. deafening silence.

Pastiche: imitation of another's work.

Pastoral: simple, rural, innocent, idyllic.

Pathetic fallacy: inanimate objects showing human attributes, e.g. the sea smiled benignly.

Personification: concrete or abstract object made human, by using a capital letter or personal pronoun, e.g. Nature.

Picaresque: low-life characters on a journey.

Post-modernism: a genre often characterised by random discontinuity, ambivalence, paradox and a self-conscious writing style.

Pun/Double entendre: a word with a double meaning, usually employed in witty wordplay but not always.

Retrospective: account of events after they have occurred.

Romanticism: genre celebrating the power of imagination, spriritualism and nature.

Semantic/lexical field: related words about a single concept, e.g. king, queen and prince are all concerned with royalty.

Style: choice of language, form and structure, and effects produced.

Synecdoche: one part of something referring to the whole, e.g. Carker's teeth represent him in *Dombey and Son*.

Syntax: the way words and sentences are placed together.

Tetracolon climax: sentence with four parts, culminating with the last part, e.g. 'I have nothing to offer but blood, toil, tears, and sweat ' (Winston Churchill).

ABOUT THE AUTHORS

Joe Broadfoot Jr is a soccer journalist, who also writes fiction and literary criticism. His former experiences as a DJ took him to far-flung places such as Tokyo, Kobe, Beijing, Hong Kong, Jakarta, Cairo, Dubai, Cannes, Oslo, Bergen and Bodo. He is now a CELTA-qualified English teacher with a first-class honours degree in Literature and an MA in Victorian Studies. David Broadfoot is studying English Literature in the Sixth Form at Thomas Tallis School and is a member of the Thomson Reuters Press Gang.

CPSIA information can be obtained at www.ICGtesting.com
Printed in the USA
LVOW12s2009060515

437467LV00024B/552/P